# GATLINBURG TRAVEL GUIDE 2023

Essential Guide for First-Time Visitors: A Comprehensive Overview of Gatlinburg, its Hidden gems, Attractions, Cuisine and day Trips for a Memorable Holiday.

By

Mark E. Fears

ALL RIGHTS RESERVED.

No part of this publication may be reproduced, distributed or transmitted in any form or by any means including photocopying, recording or other electronic or mechanical methods without the prior written permission of the publisher, except in the case of brief quotations embedded in critical reviews and certain other noncommercial uses permitted by copyright law.

Copyright © Mark E. Fears, 2023

Table of Contents

Introduction

Brief History

Religion

Customs and Culture

Geography

**Chapter 1: Basic Travel Tips**

1. When to travel

2. How to get to Gatlinburg

3. The Ideal Time to Visit

4. What to do when you get there

5. Best hotels to stay when you get there

**Chapter 2: Planning Your Trip**

1. Requirements for Entry

2. Types of Visas for Travelers

3. Limitations on Travel

4. What to bring

**Chapter 3: Gatlinburg's Transportation And Accomodation Options**

1. Getting Around
2. Accommodation Options
   1. Hotels and Resorts:
   2. Chalets and Cabins
   3. Hotels and B&Bs
   4. Campgrounds and RV resorts

**Chapter 4: Gatlinburg's Currency**

1. Gatlinburg Dollar
2. Where to Find Money Exchange
3. Budgeting & Money

**Chapter 5: Gatlinburg Language**

1. Gatlinburg English
2. language Expressions

**Chapter 6: Gatlinburg's Attractions**

1. Great Smoky Mountains National Park
2. Ober Gatlinburg
3. Skylift Park in Gatlinburg:
4. Smokies' version of Ripley's Aquarium:
5. Space Needle in Gatlinburg:

6. Hollywood star automobile museum
7. Gatlinburg's artistic community:
8. A mountain coaster in Gatlinburg:
9. Fun on Gatlin's Smoky Mountain:

## Chapter 7: Outdoor Recreations
1. Paths for Nature Hikes:
2. Observing Wildlife
3. Fishing:
4. Rafting in Whitewater
5. Ziplining:
6. Mounted Riding:
7. Golfing:
8. Snowboarding and Skiing:

## Chapter 8: Dining and shopping
1. Shopping in Gatlinburg's Downtown:
2. The local Stores:
3. Loop for Arts & Crafts:
4. Farmers' Market in Gatlinburg:
5. Restaurants and Regional Food:
6. Distilleries and Breweries:

## Chapter 9: Festivals and Events

1. Fourth of July midnight procession in Gatlinburg:

2. Winter Wonder in Gatlinburg:

3. Songs and legends from the Smoky Mountains:

4. Fair of Craftspeople in Gatlinburg:

5. Chilli Cook-off in Gatlinburg:

6. Wildflower Pilgrimage in Spring:

## Chapter 10: Gatlinburg Day Trips

1. Pigeon Forge

2. Disney World

3. Cades Cove

4. Clingmans Dome

5. The Arts and Crafts Loop in Gatlinburg

## Chapter 11: Security And Safety

1. General Travel Tips:

2. Security Precautions:

# Introduction

Gatlinburg is a picturesque mountain town that enchants visitors with its natural beauty, outdoor adventures, and lively atmosphere. It is located right in the middle of the Great Smoky Mountains. Gatlinburg, which is situated in eastern Tennessee, is a popular entry point to the famed Great Smoky Mountains National Park. Millions of tourists come here every year to explore the stunning landscapes and take in the area's rich cultural history.

Due to the nearby mountain ranges, which serve as sentinels of the natural grandeur, Gatlinburg immediately exudes a sense of calmness and peace as you enter the city. You are invited to immerse yourself in nature's wonders by towering peaks, lush woods, and gushing waterfalls. With their ethereal blue haze that covers the horizon, the Great Smoky Mountains create a magical backdrop that appears to exist outside of time. The area's extensive natural resources offer outdoor enthusiasts a playground with options for hiking, fishing, bicycling, camping, and other activities. The Great Smoky

Mountains National Park offers a variety of opportunities for both inexperienced and experienced adventurers with its more than 800 miles of trails.

In addition to its stunning natural surroundings, Gatlinburg has a bustling downtown center filled with stores, eateries, and attractions. The Parkway, the town's main avenue, is lined with attractive shops, galleries, and specialized stores where tourists may purchase one-of-a-kind items created in the area as well as original crafts and artwork. The eclectic culinary scene, which combines traditional Southern cuisine with foreign flavors, will thrill foodies.

Ober Gatlinburg, a ski resort and entertainment park perched on a mountain and reached by a picturesque aerial tramway, is one of Gatlinburg's most recognizable sights. Visitors can go on exhilarating rides, go ice skating, see wildlife, and during the winter months, even hit the slopes. The park provides all-year-round activities and sweeping views of the mountains nearby.

Gatlinburg provides a window into the area's rich history and culture for people who are interested in these subjects. The greatest collection of independent artists in North America may be found in the Great Smoky Arts & Crafts Community, which is situated just outside the town. Explore the many art galleries, studios, and craft stores in the area to see how traditional Appalachian crafts are made and to buy one-of-a-kind handmade products.

Gatlinburg also holds many annual celebrations and events that highlight the town's vivacious character and culture. A few examples of the town's busy event calendar include the Gatlinburg Craftsmen's Fair, Gatlinburg Chili Cook-Off, and the Great Smoky Easter Arts & Crafts Show.

## Brief History

Gatlinburg, located in Tennessee's stunning Smoky Mountains, is a community with a long and fascinating history. Gatlinburg has seen a fascinating evolution over time, from the early Native American occupants to its metamorphosis into a well-liked tourist resort.

Long before European inhabitants came to the area, Gatlinburg's history began. The Cherokee people, who prospered in the lush grounds around the Pigeon River, were the first inhabitants of the region. They founded a settlement called "Shining Rock" and made use of the rich natural resources for commerce and subsistence.

The first European settlers entered the region in the late 18th century. One of them was William Ogle, who arrived in the region at the beginning of the 19th century and erected a cabin close to the meeting point of the West Fork and Middle Fork of the Little Pigeon River. Sadly, William Ogle passed away soon after he arrived, and his widow, Martha Jane Huskey Ogle, rose to prominence in the community.

The settlement grew as new people arrived. Radford Gatlin, a clergyman, and trader who came to the region in the 1850s, is largely responsible for Gatlinburg's early prosperity. Gatlin helped the local economy thrive by establishing a general store, a post office, and even a sawmill.

Gatlin's outspokenness and involvement in political disputes, however, created conflicts in the neighborhood. Gatlin was eventually expelled from the area by a vote of the locals, and his name was wiped off the town's official records, giving rise to the term "Gatlinburg."

The building of the Knoxville and Charleston Railroad in the late 19th century improved accessibility to the area and accelerated Gatlinburg's development. Due to the region's extensive woods, which offered plenty of resources for logging and sawmills, the timber industry grew to be a substantial economic force. For many years, logging operations supported the local economy.

The surrounding area was included in the creation of the Great Smoky Mountains National Park in the early 20th century. The park's natural beauty and a plethora of species attracted a fresh wave of tourists to Gatlinburg as a result of this classification. The formation of the park helped to preserve the area's natural ecology and offered chances for tourism and outdoor leisure.

Through the 20th century, Gatlinburg's appeal as a tourist destination grew. The city's central business district expanded and now has a wide range of stores, eateries, and activities. The ski resort and theme park Ober Gatlinburg opened in 1962, significantly enhancing the city's allure and drawing tourists all year long.

Tragically, a terrible wildfire that ravaged the area in November 2016 presented Gatlinburg with a serious obstacle. The firestorm, often known as the "Great Smoky Mountains wildfires," claimed many homes, businesses, and people. However, the neighborhood showed resiliency and banded together to help individuals who were impacted and rebuild.

Gatlinburg has maintained its popularity as a vacation destination in recent years. Numerous attractions are available in the city, including Ripley's Believe It or Not!

the Gatlinburg Space Needle, a museum, and a variety of outdoor pursuits like hiking, fishing, and wildlife observation. Gatlinburg's appeal is also enhanced by the local Appalachian culture, which is represented in crafts, music, and cuisine.

Gatlinburg still endures as proof of the community's tenacity and the splendor of the area's natural surroundings. Travelers looking for adventure and relaxation in the majesty of the Smoky Mountains adore it for its rich history as well as its contemporary conveniences and attractions.

## Religion

Gatlinburg's cultural and social fabric has been significantly shaped by religion throughout its history. The community of the city, which is part of the Bible Belt region of the United States, has been shaped by several different religious traditions.

Gatlinburg had a significant religious presence from the time it was first settled. Many of the original European inhabitants in the region were fervent believers who brought their religion with them. Christianity was the most common religion in the area, with Baptist, Methodist, and Presbyterian faiths gaining ground there. Early settlers frequently congregated in little log churches for communal meetings and religious ceremonies.

Churches played a significant role in the development of Gatlinburg as the city evolved and became increasingly well-known. The religious institutions acted as community social and cultural hubs in addition to offering spiritual direction. They gave people a sense of cohesion and camaraderie, enabling them to band together and assist one another.

Gatlinburg has seen the emergence of numerous churches and religious institutions over time. Congregational variety increased, reflecting the city's citizens' varied upbringings and worldviews. Along with the usual Protestant churches, Gatlinburg also has Catholic, Lutheran, Episcopal, and Pentecostal churches.

Gatlinburg's surroundings, the Great Smoky Mountains National Park, have also affected the local religious scene. Religious organizations seeking solitude in nature and spiritual retreats have been drawn to the area by its unspoiled natural beauty. There are many retreat centers and campgrounds in the area that offer venues for religious events, conferences, and outdoor worship sessions.

Additionally, Gatlinburg's religious organizations have been actively involved in giving back to the community and serving others. Churches have played a significant role in helping the less fortunate, planning philanthropic events, and taking part in community improvement projects. These initiatives have helped the locals develop a sense of solidarity, compassion, and social responsibility.

The cultural calendar of Gatlinburg also includes important religious celebrations and occasions. Special occasions, parades, and gatherings are held to commemorate religious holidays like Christmas and Easter. These events serve as chances for the community to come together and celebrate their shared faith in addition to having religious importance.

The moral and ethical standards of the city reflect the impact of religion. The values emphasized by religious institutions, including those of honesty, compassion, and kindness, have contributed to the development of Gatlinburg's character. This has helped to build the city's reputation as a pleasant and hospitable tourist destination.

Though Christianity still predominates in Gatlinburg, it is important to note that the city has recently witnessed a rise in religious diversity. People from various religious origins have settled in Gatlinburg as the population has increased and diversified. This variety has enriched the city's religious tapestry, enriched its cultural landscape, and promoted interfaith communication and understanding.

## Customs and Culture

Gatlinburg's history, natural beauty, and citizens' varied origins all play a significant role in the city's culture and traditions. The cultural fabric of this thriving city has evolved through time as a result of a distinctive fusion of Appalachian, Southern, and tourist influences.

The strong sense of community in Gatlinburg is one of its defining characteristics. The people of Gatlinburg take great pride in their friendly neighborhood and actively engage in a range of charitable, cultural, and social events. The community spirit is evident in everything from volunteering at neighborhood activities to patronizing nearby shops and craftspeople.

Gatlinburg's cultural character places a specific emphasis on its Appalachian history. The city celebrates and upholds the legacy of the Appalachian region by embracing its customs, crafts, and music. Visitors can see experienced craftsmen presenting their products at neighborhood stores and marketplaces. Traditional crafts including carpentry, basket weaving, quilting, and pottery have been passed down through generations.

Another essential component of Gatlinburg's cultural fabric is Appalachian music. Talented musicians frequently play live shows for locals and tourists alike, filling the streets and venues with bluegrass, folk, and country music. The air is filled with the sounds of banjos, fiddles, and mandolins, attracting listeners and preserving the local musical traditions.

Gatlinburg also values its Southern roots, which can be seen in the city's cuisine and friendliness. Many neighborhood eateries offer a sense of traditional Southern flavors by serving Southern comfort food like fried chicken, cornbread, collard greens, and pecan pie. The hospitality of the Gatlinburg residents shows off their warmth and friendliness, making guests feel at home and well looked after.

The city's popularity as a tourist destination has also influenced its cultural landscape. Gatlinburg welcomes millions of tourists annually, and its culture has changed to accept and accommodate this increase in visitors. A thriving tourism business has sprung up alongside the traditional Appalachian and Southern influences, providing a variety of activities, entertainment, and facilities.

The Gatlinburg Space Needle, the Gatlinburg SkyLift, and Ripley's Aquarium of the Smokies are just a few of the famous tourist destinations that have come to represent the city. Visitors can partake in a range of outdoor activities, explore museums, take in live entertainment, ride exhilarating amusement rides, and more. Gatlinburg's culture has evolved to offer activities and encounters that satisfy a wide range of tourist interests.

Gatlinburg holds a lot of festivals and events all year long that highlight its customs and culture. The Smoky Mountain Tunes and Tales event invites musicians, storytellers, and street performers to the city's streets, providing a window into the area's rich history. The Great Smoky Arts & Crafts Community displays handcrafted goods, original artwork, and other works by local artisans.

With occasions like Winterfest, the Gatlinburg Craftsmen's Fair, and the Smoky Mountain Harvest Festival, Gatlinburg also embraces seasonal celebrations. These events celebrate the passing of the seasons and provide guests and locals the chance to fully experience the city's cultural attractions.

Gatlinburg's cultural identity is influenced by its natural environment in addition to these cultural celebrations. Hiking, wildlife viewing, and outdoor concerts are just a few of the cultural pursuits that take place against the backdrop of the Great Smoky Mountains National Park. The park's unblemished beauty and conservation initiatives highlight how crucial it is to protect the natural legacy for future generations.

# Geography

Eastern Tennessee's Gatlinburg is tucked away amid the gorgeous Great Smoky Mountains. Its geography is determined by how close it is to the area's natural attractions, such as the mountains, rivers, and forests around the city.

The geographic location of Gatlinburg within the Great Smoky Mountains is one of its distinguishing characteristics. These Appalachian Mountains, which are a portion of a bigger mountain range, are renowned for their historic peaks, lush forests, and rich wildlife. The Great Smoky Mountains National Park, which covers more than 500,000 acres and is famous for its natural splendor, has Gatlinburg as its gateway.

The Pigeon River runs through the center of the city, which is situated in Sevier County. The river and its tributaries enhance the region's natural beauty and offer chances for water sports including kayaking, rafting, and fishing.

The dense forest that surrounds Gatlinburg is largely made up of hardwood trees including oak, hickory, and maple. In the autumn, when the leaves change into a magnificent display of red, orange, and gold, these woodlands are especially bright. The region's lush vegetation also provides a habitat for a wide variety of plant and animal species, adding to its ecological importance.

The actual city is tucked away in a valley between two enormous mountain ranges. The most noteworthy of these mountains are the Great Smoky Mountains' second-highest peak, Mount Guyot, Mount LeConte, and Clingmans Dome. The mountains offer chances for hiking, camping, and enjoying the area's natural marvels in addition to offering breathtaking panoramic vistas.

The location of Gatlinburg concerning the Tennessee-North Carolina border has an impact on its landscape as well. Due to the city's proximity to the state line, both inhabitants and guests can readily reach both states' tourist destinations and natural areas. The Eastern

Band of Cherokee Indians, who reside in Cherokee, North Carolina, a nearby town, provide an insight into the area's extensive Native American legacy.

There are four different seasons in Gatlinburg's humid subtropical climate. Summers are typically hot and muggy, with highs in the 80s and sporadic afternoon thunderstorms. Visitors come from all over due to the milder temperatures and colorful foliage that fall provides. The seasons of spring and winter are pleasant with occasional snowfall in higher elevations during the mild to cool winters.

# Chapter 1: Basic Travel Tips

## 1. When to Travel

There are many things to think about when organizing a trip to Gatlinburg, Tennessee, to maximize your experience there. The Great Smoky Mountains Gatlinburg is a quaint mountain town with a wealth of recreational opportunities, scenic views, and cultural experiences. Let's look at the various times of the year and events to assist you choose when to travel.

**Spring Time (March to May:)**
Gatlinburg's springtime is a lovely time of year as wildlife emerges from its winter hibernation. The weather is nice, and the temperature is rising gradually. It's the perfect time of year to go hiking and explore the many paths in the Great Smoky Mountains because of how colorful the wildflowers are. The Spring Wildflower Pilgrimage, a week-long celebration of the region's flora and fauna, takes place in April. It includes guided walks, lectures, and workshops.

**Summertime (June through August)**

In Gatlinburg, the summer is the busiest travel period, and with good reason. The pleasant weather is ideal for outdoor activities. You can go zip-lining through the lush green canopy or hiking, fishing, whitewater rafting, or all of the above. The Gatlinburg Craftsmen's Fair, which features regional craftsmen and their works, is just one of the many events and attractions taking place in the area. Remember that summer might be crowded, so it's best to reserve lodging and activities in advance.

**September to November:**

The breathtaking autumn foliage in Gatlinburg draws tourists from all over the world. The scenery is breathtaking as the leaves change into brilliant hues of red, orange, and gold. A must-do when visiting the Great Smoky Mountains National Park is to take one of the scenic drives, including the Newfound Gap Road or the Roaring Fork Motor Nature Trail. The Smoky Mountain Harvest Festival, which features regional food, music, and craft events, is another festival held in Gatlinburg.

**December through February is winter.**

Gatlinburg's attractiveness is different in the winter. With snow-capped peaks and holiday decorations lining the streets, the town is transformed into a winter wonderland. The town's ski resort and amusement park, Ober Gatlinburg, is the perfect place to go skiing, snowboarding, and ice skating at this time of year. With the Winter Magic Trolley Ride of Lights, an enchanted tour that features millions of glittering Christmas lights, the Great Smoky Mountains become even more alluring in December.

When determining when to visit Gatlinburg, take into account aspects outside the seasons like your budget, personal tastes, and events of interest. Keep in mind that weekdays and shoulder seasons are better if you want a quieter experience because weekends, holidays, and special events tend to be busier. Gatlinburg provides a plethora of scenic beauty, outdoor adventures, and cultural encounters that will leave you with priceless memories whenever you visit.

## 2. How to get to Gatlinburg

Gatlinburg, Tennessee, offers a variety of transportation alternatives to fit your interests and needs, making getting there an exciting aspect of planning your vacation. Here are some options for getting around, whether you like driving, flying, or taking public transportation:

**By Air:**

McGhee Tyson Airport (TYS), located about 45 miles from Gatlinburg in Knoxville, Tennessee, is the closest significant airport. Regular flights to and from this airport are offered by several significant airlines, making it a practical choice for travelers. To get to Gatlinburg from the airport, you can either rent a car or use a shuttle. Airport transportation services are also provided by a few local hotels and resorts.

**By Car:**

Many people choose to drive to Gatlinburg, especially those who prefer road vacations and having the freedom to take their time and discover the gorgeous routes. Interstate 40 and Interstate 75, two of the main thoroughfares, are both convenient for reaching the town. You can take indicated routes that take you straight to Gatlinburg from cities like Knoxville, Nashville, or Asheville. Remember that the area's mountain roads can be winding and steep; use caution when driving, especially when it's raining or snowing.

**By Bus:**

Numerous bus companies offer service to Gatlinburg and the surrounding area if you want to go by bus. Two well-known bus companies, Greyhound and Megabus, provide routes to Knoxville, from whence you can board a regional bus or make other travel arrangements to Gatlinburg. A few tour companies and travel businesses also provide guided bus trips that include Gatlinburg in their itineraries.

**In a train:**

Although there isn't a direct train line from the train station in Knoxville or Asheville to Gatlinburg, you can use Amtrak to travel to one of these adjacent cities, continue by bus or rent a car to get to Gatlinburg. Amtrak provides comfortable travel alternatives and scenic routes, letting you take in the beautiful scenery while you travel.

**Using a motorcycle**

Riding a motorcycle to Gatlinburg can be a thrilling experience for motorcycling aficionados. The hamlet is close to the gorgeous Tail of the Dragon and the famed Blue Ridge Parkway, which provide motorcycle riders with spectacular views and exhilarating curving roads. As a result of the availability of lodgings that welcome motorcycles, the region is a favorite among motorcyclists looking for an unforgettable journey.

Once you get to Gatlinburg, you may either rent a car to have the freedom to explore the nearby Great Smoky Mountains or use public transit like taxis or trolleys to get around town. When selecting the mode of transportation that suits you best, take into account your travel preferences, financial limitations, and time limits.

Gatlinburg welcomes guests with its unmatched natural beauty, inviting environment, and variety of activities to make your trip unforgettable, regardless of how you get there.

## 3. The Ideal Time to Visit

Depending on your particular preferences and the experiences you're looking for, you can decide what time of year is best to visit Gatlinburg, Tennessee. Let's examine the highlights of each season to aid in your decision-making because each one has its special attractions and activities:

**March to May:**
In Gatlinburg, spring offers blossoming wildflowers, comfortable temperatures, and a feeling of renewal. It's the perfect time to go trekking and explore the outdoors since the Great Smoky Mountains are alive with vibrant blossoms. As the snow melts, you may see the emergence of colorful flora and take in flowing waterfalls. Along with offering guided walks,

educational events, and photographic workshops, the annual Spring Wildflower Pilgrimage enables you to strengthen your bond with the area's natural splendor.

**Summertime (June through August)**

Gatlinburg experiences its busiest travel season in the summer because of the pleasant weather and plenty of outdoor activities. The Great Smoky Mountains' lush vegetation serves as a setting for activities including hiking, fishing, whitewater rafting, and zip lining. Families may enjoy thrilling rides and entertainment at theme parks and water parks like Dollywood and Ober Gatlinburg. A vibrant and busy time of year to come, the town also hosts the Gatlinburg Craftsmen's Fair, which features local craftspeople demonstrating their wares.

**September to November:**

Due to its stunning foliage, fall is undoubtedly the most popular season to visit Gatlinburg. Visitors come from near and far as the mountains and trees are transformed into a colorful tapestry of reds, oranges, and yellows. Awe-inspiring views may be found along scenic drives on roads like the Newfound Gap Road and the Roaring Fork Motor Nature Trail. During this time, the Smoky Mountain Harvest Festival is held, which includes events showcasing regional cuisine, music, and crafts. Be ready.

**December through February is winter.**
Gatlinburg, Tennessee, offers a special and wonderful experience throughout the winter, highlighting the town's charm in the middle of a snow wonderland. The Great Smoky Mountains are changed into a charming winter scene that is covered with sparkling snow. Outdoor pursuits and beautiful drives are set against a breathtaking backdrop of snow-capped peaks. Visit Ober Gatlinburg, a well-known ski area and amusement park that is situated above the town.

Gatlinburg celebrates the Christmas season with many winter festivals and events, parades, live music performances, and fireworks displays. Compared to the busy summer season, Gatlinburg is more tranquil in the winter. In the winter, there are fewer people around to appreciate the town's attractions and the beauty of nature, giving you a more tranquil and pleasant experience.

## 4. What to do when you get there

There are several activities and attractions in Gatlinburg, Tennessee, to satisfy every interest and taste. Everyone can find something to enjoy in Gatlinburg, whether they are nature lovers, adventure seekers, history buffs, or foodies. Some of the best activities to do when you get there are listed below:

**1. Great Smoky Mountains National Park exploration:**
The Great Smoky Mountains are right outside Gatlinburg's door, providing countless options for outdoor pursuits. Hike along beautiful pathways, such as the well-known Appalachian Trail or the lovely Alum Cave Trail. Clingmans Dome, the park's highest peak, offers stunning vistas. Enjoy observing wildlife, going fishing, having a picnic, or just taking in the natural beauty.

**2. Ober Gatlinburg excursion:**

Take the aerial tramway from Gatlinburg's downtown to Ober Gatlinburg, a ski resort and amusement park on a hilltop. Experience wildlife interactions, snow tubing, skiing, snowboarding, and ice skating. Alpine slides, a mountain coaster, water slides, mini golf, and chairlift rides are all available during the warmer months. Along with these amenities, the park has a skating rink and retail establishments.

**3. Learn about the Gatlinburg Arts and Crafts Scene:**

Discover the Gatlinburg Arts & Crafts Community to see the largest collection of independent craftspeople in North America. Walk an 8-mile loop to see over 100 studios, galleries, and businesses run by artists. See how masterful artisans create ceramics, woodwork, jewelry, paintings, and other items. Finding one-of-a-kind items and unusual souvenirs is very easy here.

**4. Become Fully Immersed in History:**

There are several sites in Gatlinburg where you may learn about the city's history. Visit the Gatlinburg Space Needle, a viewing platform that provides sweeping panoramas of the city and the mountains. Discover the Gatlinburg Historic Ogle Log Cabin, a log cabin from the 1800s that depicts pioneer life. A visit to the Hollywood Star Cars Museum and the Salt & Pepper Shaker Museum is also recommended.

**5. Discover Ripley's Attractions:**

Gatlinburg is home to some bizarre and entertaining Ripley's attractions. Visit Ripley's Aquarium of the Smokies for intriguing exhibits on aquatic life and engaging hands-on activities. Look around at Ripley's Believe It or Not!, a museum containing strange objects and anomalies from all across the world. For more exhilarating thrills, check out Ripley's Moving Theater and Haunted Adventure.

**6. Eat some Southern food:**

There are several restaurants and cafes in Gatlinburg that serve delectable Southern food. Try traditional fare including barbecue, fried chicken, biscuits and gravy, and decadent desserts. Try some regional favorites like trout and country ham. Discover the many dining alternatives, including quaint cafes, farm-to-table restaurants, and family-run restaurants.

**7. Take in live performance:**
All ages may enjoy live entertainment in Gatlinburg. Visit the Sweet Fanny Adams Theatre for a variety show where gifted actors perform fantastic comedic skits and musical productions. Visit places like Ole Red Gatlinburg or the Smoky Mountain Brewery to catch live music performances. Magic shows, comedic acts, and musical performances are presented at the Iris Theater.

**8. Drive a Scenic Route:**
Scenic routes in the area around Gatlinburg highlight the area's natural splendor. Drive through the Great Smoky Mountains National Park along the Newfound Gap Road, which offers breathtaking vistas, overlooks, and chances to spot wildlife. Another beautiful drive that

features historical structures, waterfalls, and mountain streams is the Roaring Fork Motor Nature Trail.

# 5. Best hotels to stay when you get there

You can select from a range of lodging options in Gatlinburg, Tennessee, depending on your interests, including resorts, hotels, charming cabins, and chalets. The following are some of the best choices for your stay in Gatlinburg:

**1. Rentals of cabins:**

In the picturesque mountains of Gatlinburg, there are quaint cabin rentals. These exclusive cottages, which frequently have fireplaces, hot tubs, and breathtaking views, provide a homey and rustic experience. If you're searching for a family retreat or a romantic trip, you may pick from a variety of sizes and facilities. A variety of cabins are available to meet your needs from companies like Timber Tops Luxury Cabin Rentals and Cabins of the Smoky Mountains.

**2. Condos and chalets:**
Chalet and condo rentals are also available in Gatlinburg, offering a balance of convenience and comfort. These homes frequently have full kitchens, numerous bedrooms, and shared amenities like game rooms and swimming pools. Chalet rentals are widely available and close to the town's attractions. For a range of chalet and condo possibilities, look into businesses like Chalet Village and Diamond Mountain Rentals.

**3. Hotels and resorts:**
There are many resorts and hotels in Gatlinburg to select from if you prefer a more conventional accommodation experience. The Lodge at Buckberry Creek, The Park Vista - a DoubleTree by Hilton, and The Greystone Lodge on the River are a few of the well-liked choices. These hotels provide welcoming lodgings, conveniences like fitness centers and swimming pools, and easy access to the Great Smoky Mountains National Park.

**4. Overnight stays:**

Charming bed and breakfasts that provide a warm and customized experience may be found in Gatlinburg. These establishments frequently provide interesting, well-equipped rooms, delicious breakfasts, and a welcoming ambiance. In Gatlinburg, popular choices include the Buckhorn Inn and the Foxtrot Bed and Breakfast.

**5. RV parks and campgrounds:**

There are numerous campgrounds and RV parks in Gatlinburg for people who like to camp or vacation in RVs. Both Elkmont Campground and Smoky Bear Campground are well-liked options with beautiful settings, amenities, and outdoor recreation possibilities. Many campgrounds offer facilities including hookups, showers, and campfire pits.

**6. Unique Accommodations:**

In contrast to more typical motel options, Gatlinburg has several distinctive lodging experiences. There are treehouse rentals, glamping locations, and even themed lodging options. A wonderful and engaging stay can be had at accommodations like The Treehouse Grove at Norton Creek and Under Canvas Great Smoky Mountains.

Consider considerations like location, budget, amenities, and the size of your group when choosing your lodging. To ensure your preferred choice, it is advisable to make reservations in advance, especially during popular times of the year. No matter where you choose to stay, Gatlinburg offers a range of housing alternatives that will suit a variety of preferences and guarantee a relaxing and delightful trip to this quaint mountain town.

# Chapter 2: Planning Your Trip

## 1. Requirements for Entry

Tennessee's scenic Smoky Mountains are home to the popular tourist attraction of Gatlinburg, which is renowned for its scenic surroundings, outdoor activities, and energetic downtown. Before making vacation plans to Gatlinburg, tourists should be informed of the admission requirements as with any other travel destination. Even though Gatlinburg does not have any particular admission criteria, there are a few basic rules and things tourists should keep in mind.

**1. Travel paperwork:**

- Valid Passport: Gatlinburg welcomes travelers from abroad, but they must make sure their passports are valid for at least six months after their intended departure date. For precise visa requirements, it is best to contact the consulate or embassy of the relevant nation.

- Driver's License: Visitors from within the United States who intend to drive in Gatlinburg must have a current license issued by their nation or state.

**2. Immigration and Customs:**

- Customs Declaration: International travelers must submit a customs declaration form before entering the United States, including Gatlinburg. The declaration of specific commodities, such as food, substantial sums of money, or firearms, may be required on this form, which also contains information about the items being carried into the nation.

- Immigration processes: Foreign visitors to the United States should be ready for immigration processes when they arrive. Presenting a current passport along with a completed arrival/departure form (normally issued by the airline) is usually required. It might also be necessary for visitors to disclose information regarding the reason for their trip and how long they plan to stay.

**3. Considerations for COVID-19:**

- Travel Restrictions: Because of the COVID-19 epidemic, visitors need to be aware of any regulations or restrictions put in place by regional, state, or federal authorities. These limitations may include required testing, quarantine intervals, or immunization documentation. The most recent information can be found by visiting the official websites of relevant agencies, such as the Centers for Disease Control and Prevention (CDC) and the Gatlinburg tourism board.

- Health and Safety Measures: Visitors to Gatlinburg are urged to abide by the suggested health and safety rules, which include donning masks in public indoor areas, keeping a safe distance from others, and often washing your hands or using hand sanitizer.

**4. Considerations for transportation**
- Flights: People flying into Gatlinburg usually land at one of the airports in the area, like Asheville Regional Airport in North Carolina or McGhee Tyson Airport in Knoxville, Tennessee. Before making travel plans, it is a

good idea to verify flight schedules, ticket prices, and any airline-specific policies or procedures.

- Ground Transportation: Once in Gatlinburg, tourists can use a variety of transportation options to get around the city, including rental vehicles, taxis, shuttles, and ride-sharing services. To guarantee smooth movement throughout Gatlinburg, it is advised to make transportation plans in advance or to have a plan in place.

**5. Additional factors to consider**
- trip Insurance: Before visiting Gatlinburg or any other trip location, it is always a good idea to think about getting travel insurance. Unexpected occurrences like trip cancellations, medical problems, or missing luggage may be covered by travel insurance.

- Local Laws and Regulations: Visitors to Gatlinburg should become familiar with the city's laws and rules. This includes observing all traffic laws, parking restrictions, and any unique rules for leisure pursuits or outdoor excursions in the Smoky Mountains.

It is crucial to remember that admission standards and travel recommendations might alter over time, especially in response to outside causes like public health emergencies. To stay updated about any updates or changes to the entrance criteria for Gatlinburg, it is advised for tourists to often check official government websites, consult with travel agents or local authorities, and so on.

## 2. Types of Visas for Travelers

There are many sorts of traveler's visas available for travelers in Gatlinburg, Tennessee, depending on the purpose of the trip. These visas enable visitors from various nations to go to Gatlinburg and remain there for predetermined amounts of time. The following are some examples of frequent traveler visas that one could come across:

**1. Business Visitor Visa:**

Individuals visiting Gatlinburg for business are eligible for the business visa. It enables guests to carry out tasks like going to conferences, making deals, being present at business meetings, or doing research. However, it forbids anyone from working or receiving compensation while they are in the country.

**2. Visitor on Vacation visa:**

This visa is intended for tourists and anyone visiting Gatlinburg for leisure purposes. It is appropriate for anyone who wants to take in the natural splendor of the Smoky Mountains, visit sites, go to cultural events, or just hang out with friends and family. The visitor on a vacation visa is often issued for a brief length of time and does not permit holders to work.

**3. Student Visa:**

For students who want to pursue academic courses in Gatlinburg, there is a student visa. International students attending educational institutions in Gatlinburg, including colleges or universities, frequently use this visa. It obligates people to continue their status as full-time students and might permit some restricted employment options on campus.

**4. Exchange Visa:**

Individuals engaging in recognized exchange programs in Gatlinburg are eligible for the exchange visa. Internships, research projects, and cultural and educational exchanges are a few examples of these programs. People with a exchange visa are frequently required to spend some time in their home country when the program is over.

**5. Work Visa:**

The work visa is for people who have been given an employment offer in the United States and who have specific knowledge or abilities. If your business has sponsored you and you have a job lined up in Gatlinburg, you might need to apply for the work visa.

**6. Temporary Non-Agricultural Worker Visa:**

This visa is for people looking for short-term, non-agricultural employment possibilities in Gatlinburg. People who work in seasonal industries like hospitality, tourism, or construction frequently use this visa type. Employers must show a need for temporary workers and follow all applicable labor laws.

**7. Investor Visa:**

People from nations that have a treaty of commerce and navigation with the United States are eligible for the investor visa. It enables business owners and investors to launch or run a company in Gatlinburg. Individuals must make a sizable investment and actively participate in business activities to be eligible for an investor visa.

**8. The VWP (Visa Waiver Program):**

The Visa Waiver Program enables nationals of specific nations to travel or conduct business in the United States, including Gatlinburg, without needing to obtain a conventional visa. The Electronic System for Travel Authorization (ESTA) is a pre-trip requirement for travelers covered by the VWP.

It is essential to contact the nearest American embassy or consulate in your country or to go to the American government's official website. To find out the precise visa requirements for your nationality and travel objectives, contact the Department of State. Depending on the type of visa, there may be differences in the application procedure, required paperwork, and fees. To ensure enough processing time, it is advised to start the visa application procedure well in advance.

It is important to stay current on the most recent information and instructions issued by the U.S. government authorities because visa restrictions and requirements can change.

## 3. Limitations on Travel

As far as I am aware, Gatlinburg, Tennessee, will not have any special travel limitations that only apply to tourists. It is crucial to keep in mind that travel limitations and policies might alter over time, particularly in response to outside circumstances like public health emergencies. Therefore, before making travel arrangements to Gatlinburg, visitors need to keep up with any updates or modifications to the applicable travel restrictions. Here are some common things to think about when it comes to travel restrictions:

**1. Considerations for COVID-19:**
- Pandemic guidelines: During the COVID-19 pandemic, municipal, state, and federal authorities have all implemented travel restrictions and advice. These rules may include necessary testing, mandated quarantine times, or immunization documentation. Visitors must constantly be aware of the most recent recommendations made by the U.S. Centers for Disease Control and Prevention (CDC). local health departments and the Department of State.

- Entry criteria: There may be particular entry criteria associated with COVID-19 depending on the visitor's country of origin. This can entail submitting a negative PCR or antigen test result obtained within a certain window of time before arrival, filling out health declaration paperwork, or passing through airport health checks.

- Mask Requirements and Social Distancing: Travelers visiting Gatlinburg should be aware of any local laws requiring the wearing of masks or enforcing social segregation. These actions could change and vary depending on the local COVID-19 scenario at the time.

**2. Visa and immigration restrictions:**
- Visa and immigration limitations may apply to travelers from specific nations while entering the United States. Visitors to Gatlinburg must confirm the exact visa requirements related to their nationality and the reason for their trip. They can get this information through the U.S. or from the closest American embassy or consulate in their nation. the main website of the Department of State.

**3. Travel Warnings:**
- On occasion, government organizations may issue travel warnings to alert tourists to possible dangers or

risks in a certain location. Before traveling, tourists should look up any Gatlinburg-related travel warnings or alerts. These warnings could relate to a variety of things, like safety issues, natural disasters, or political unrest.

**4. Limitations on Transportation:**

- Any transportation constraints that can have an impact on visitors' travel arrangements should also be taken into account. Flight restrictions, service cancellations, or schedule modifications for public transit are just a few examples of these limits. For any updates or changes in services, it is advisable to verify with the appropriate transportation authorities or airlines.

**5. Regional Rules:**

- Before arriving in Gatlinburg, visitors should get familiar with any laws or ordinances that could affect how they travel. This can include obeying traffic regulations, observing parking restrictions, and abiding by any particular standards or norms on local leisure pursuits, such as hiking or camping in the Smoky Mountains.

Visitors are advised to often check official government websites, speak with travel professionals or local officials, and stay informed of any updates or changes to the Gatlinburg travel restrictions to ensure a smooth and hassle-free journey. Visitors can have a pleasant and responsible trip by being prepared and according to the rules.

## 4. What to bring

It's crucial to carry the appropriate necessities for a comfortable and enjoyable journey when getting ready for a trip to Gatlinburg, Tennessee. Here are some broad tips for what to bring for various genders and kids, while specific items may vary depending on personal tastes and the time of year you want to visit:

**For All Ages and Genders:**
1. Clothing:
- Comfy walking shoes for touring Gatlinburg's outdoors and downtown.

- Seasonally appropriate lightweight and breathable apparel, such as t-shirts, shorts, or dresses for warm weather and sweaters or coats for colder weather.

- Rain gear, including a waterproof jacket or umbrella, as Gatlinburg's weather may be erratic.

**2. Personal Hygiene:**
- Toiletries such as toothpaste, shampoo, conditioner, and any other personal care products you might require.

- Lip balm and sunscreen to prevent sunburn, especially when participating in outdoor activities.

- Use insect repellent to protect yourself from mosquitoes and other biting insects.

**3. Entertainment and electronic devices:**
- Cell phones, chargers, and any other necessary electronic equipment.

- Cameras or camcorders to record Gatlinburg's and the Smoky Mountains' stunning landscape.

- Reading materials like books or periodicals or other leisure activities.

**For men's:**
**1. Clothing:**
- Comfortable shirts with long and short sleeves for various weather conditions.

- Jeans or shorts, according to the occasion and the wearer's desire.

- Swimwear if you intend to visit water parks or take a dip.

**2. Accessories:**
- Sunscreen-protective hats or caps.

- Sunglasses to safeguard your eyes.

- A thin sweater or jacket for chilly evenings.

**For ladies:**

**1. Clothing:**

- Comfy shorts or pants, as well as dresses or skirts.

- A selection of tops and blouses that may be mixed and matched.

- Swimwear if you intend to visit water parks or take a dip.

**2. Accessories:**

- Scarves or wraps for styling purposes or layering.

- Accessorize with jewelry and other items to complete your looks.

- A multipurpose handbag or backpack to transport necessities while traveling.

**For young people:**

**1. Clothing:**

- Comfy clothes that are suited for the temperature, like t-shirts, shorts, slacks, and thin coats or sweaters.

- Swimwear for activities in the water.

- Extra clothing, especially for younger children, in case of spills or mishaps.

**2. Personal Hygiene**:

- Diapers, wipes, and any other baby care supplies required for young children.

- Age-appropriate insect repellant and sunscreen for kids.

**3. Amusement and comfort**

- Favorite games, novels, or toys to occupy kids during downtime and travel.

- Snacks and beverages to keep kids energized throughout the journey.

- Solaces like a favorite blanket or cuddly animal to evoke feelings of familiarity.

When preparing for Gatlinburg, keep in mind the unique requirements and preferences of your family members. It's also a good idea to check the weather forecast before your journey to make sure you've dressed appropriately for the weather. You'll be able to move around more easily and have everything you need for a relaxing trip to Gatlinburg if you pack small, adaptable goods.

# Chapter 3: Gatlinburg's Transportation And Accomodation Options

## 1. Getting Around

Gatlinburg, a lovely mountain town tucked in the center of the Great Smoky Mountains, offers guests a variety of transportation options for getting around. Here is a detailed guide to help you get around and enjoy your time in this lovely location, whether you're exploring the charming streets of downtown Gatlinburg, exploring the adjacent natural beauties, or visiting nearby attractions.

**1. Walking:**

Walking is one of the most enjoyable ways to explore Gatlinburg. The town is small and convenient for walking, with well-kept walkways and a lively environment. Walking gives you the chance to experience the distinctive atmosphere, browse specialty stores, and find hidden jewels nestled away in the back alleys and side streets. Numerous sights, eateries, and entertainment venues are close by and accessible on foot.

**2. Transport System:**

Gatlinburg has a town-wide trolley system that runs quickly and conveniently. The trolleys are a great option for transportation, especially if you don't like to walk large distances. The Downtown Parkway, Arts and Crafts Community, and National Park paths are just a few of the options. The trolleys offer a stress-free way to visit different areas of Gatlinburg because they operate frequently and are cheaply priced.

**3. Car:**

Driving about Gatlinburg gives you greater flexibility and liberty if you own or are renting a car. The town's roadways are kept up, and there are some parking options available, including parking lots and street meters. It's important to keep in mind that parking can be scarce during busy times, so if you anticipate heavy traffic, it's best to arrive early or think about other choices for getting around.

**4. Biking:**

Biking is a common way to go around Gatlinburg and the neighboring areas for those who enjoy the outdoors and the natural world. The municipality offers safe and fun biking thanks to its designated bike lanes and bike-friendly pathways. From some local outfitters, you may rent bicycles to explore the area's beautiful routes, including the Gatlinburg Trail, which links the town to the Great Smoky Mountains National Park.

**5. Services for sharing rides:**

Uber and Lyft, two well-known ride-sharing services, operate in Gatlinburg. These transportation options are practical, especially if you value the ease of door-to-door pick-up and drop-off. You can call for a ride and be taken to your location with just a few taps on your smartphone.

**6. Transport Services:**

In Gatlinburg, certain hotels and resorts provide their visitors with free shuttle services. It's a good idea to ask about the shuttles' availability and schedule if you're staying at one of these places. This service may be a practical method to get around town and see surrounding sites without having to worry about parking or figuring out new roads.

**7. Carriages carried by horses**

Horse-drawn carriages are available in downtown Gatlinburg for a dash of vintage charm. These classic rides provide a special chance to appreciate the town's beautiful charm at a relaxed pace. A charming and romantic way to see Gatlinburg is via horse-drawn carriage, especially at night when the town is illuminated by sparkling lights.

**8. Tours for sightseeing:**

Gatlinburg provides a variety of sightseeing excursions that let you unwind, take in the scenery, and learn about the region's natural treasures and history from experienced tour operators. These excursions provide a distinctive approach to discovering Gatlinburg and the surrounding mountains, whether it is a breathtaking helicopter trip, a journey on a mountain tram, or a guided bus tour.

**9. Aerial trams and Funiculars**

You can ride one of the town's aerial trams or funiculars to get sweeping views of Gatlinburg and the mountains around. For instance, the Ober Gatlinburg Aerial Tramway offers a breathtaking 2.1-mile journey from the heart of Gatlinburg to Ober Gatlinburg, a well-known ski resort and theme park. These modes of transportation combine ease with breathtaking landscapes.

# 2. Accommodation Options

### 1. Hotels and Resorts:

1. The Lodge at Buckberry Creek is a luxurious and rustic mountain getaway that is situated on a tranquil mountainside. The huge suites and private cottages at this opulent resort offer stunning views of the Smoky Mountains. Gourmet food is served in the on-site

restaurant at The Lodge, and the resort offers quick access to hiking trails and other outdoor activities.

2. Jimmy Buffett's carefree way of life served as the inspiration for Margaritaville Resort Gatlinburg, which offers a tropical haven in the middle of the mountains. A rooftop pool, a full-service spa, and a range of dining options are just a few of the attractions offered by this family-friendly resort. Visitors can experience the attractions and entertainment in downtown Gatlinburg thanks to the resort's accessible location.

3. The Park Vista, a DoubleTree by Hilton hotel, offers breathtaking panoramic views of Gatlinburg and the nearby mountains from its vantage point overlooking the city. The hotel features a picturesque restaurant, an indoor pool, a fitness facility, and rooms that are both spacious and pleasant. It is ideally situated close to well-known attractions including the Great Smoky Mountains National Park and Ripley's Aquarium of the Smokies.

4. Gatlinburg Inn: The Gatlinburg Inn is a great option if you're seeking a historic hotel with a dash of Southern friendliness. At the gateway to the Great Smoky Mountains National Park sits this lovely monument, built in 1937. The inn is a great starting point for exploring the nearby natural wonders and boutiques because of its pleasant rooms, rocking chairs on the porch, and close access to downtown Gatlinburg.

5. Families will love the Westgate Smoky Mountain Resort & Water Park, which has a variety of lodging options, including cabins and villas. The vast site has a water park, many pools, mini-golf, and several recreational pursuits. Although the resort is located in a tranquil mountain setting, Gatlinburg's busiest attractions are only a short drive away.

6. The Lodge at Buckberry Creek is a boutique lodge in the Smoky Mountains that offers a tranquil escape with a blend of rustic beauty and contemporary comforts. The resort offers the perfect environment for rest and renewal with its roomy accommodations, superb dining options,

and large outdoor areas. Additionally, it provides easy access to fly fishing, hiking trails, and other outdoor activities.

7. Glenstone Lodge: Glenstone Lodge is a full-service hotel with spacious grounds and comfortable accommodations that provides a variety of amenities. Visitors can take advantage of the hotel's indoor and outdoor pools, fitness center, on-site restaurant, and even wedding chapel. The hotel's convenient location makes it simple to reach Ober Gatlinburg Ski Resort and Amusement Park as well as other Gatlinburg attractions.

8. The Inn at Christmas Place offers a year-round holiday environment for guests looking for a distinctive and joyous experience. This Bavarian-inspired hotel is close to the Great Smoky Mountains National Park and is decked out for the holidays. It has warm rooms, a heated outdoor pool, a Bavarian-style bakery, and a big lobby with a huge Christmas tree.

## 2. Chalets and Cabins

**1. Smokey Bear campsite:** A family-friendly campsite with a variety of camping options, Smoky Bear Campground is within a short distance from the heart of Gatlinburg. They rent out lovely cabins, roomy tent sites, and RV sites with all the hookups. There are facilities in the campground, including swimming pools, playgrounds, laundries, and a camp store. Smoky Bear Campground is a well-liked option for those wanting to explore the area because of its handy location and well-kept amenities.

**2. RVers** can find a serene and beautiful location at Twin Creek RV Resort, which is located on the banks of Little Pigeon River. Full-hookup RV sites are available at the resort, along with many extras like cable TV, fire pits, and picnic tables. The swimming pool, campfire, and fishing in the river are all available to visitors. Twin Creek RV Resort is the perfect starting point for outdoor experiences due to its proximity to the national park and stunning surroundings.

**3. Greenbrier Campground** is a lovely campground that offers a peaceful and natural camping experience. It is located right in the middle of the Smoky Mountains. Tent sites and full-hookup RV sites are both available at the campsite, several of which are close to the river. Trails for hiking, fishing, and river swimming are available for visitors. The peaceful ambiance of the campground and its proximity to scenic routes and hiking trails make it a favorite among outdoor enthusiasts.

**4. Camp LeConte Luxury Outdoor Resort:** Camp LeConte Luxury Outdoor Resort is a great option for people looking for a distinctive camping experience with a dash of luxury. This upmarket campground provides a variety of lodging choices, including tent sites, RV sites with full hookups, and safari tents and treehouses designed for glamping. A swimming pool, a camp store, a game room, and organized activities are among the resort's facilities. Camping in Camp LeConte is a remarkable experience thanks to the harmony of nature and convenience.

## 3. Hotels and B&Bs

Bed and breakfasts in Gatlinburg are a great alternative if you're looking for a more private and homey lodging option. These places provide a tailored experience, cozy lodgings, and a sumptuous prepared breakfast to get your day started.

**1. Buckhorn Inn** is a historic bed & breakfast renowned for its old-world beauty and welcoming hospitality. It is tucked away in the peaceful foothills of the Smoky Mountains. The inn provides a range of lodging options, including comfortable rooms in the main house and exclusive cottages dispersed over the grounds. Homemade breakfast, afternoon tea, and elegant dinners are available to guests. For those who love the outdoors, the picturesque views and lovely gardens at Buckhorn Inn offer a tranquil haven.

**2. Laurel Springs Lodge** Bed and Breakfast is a delightful bed and breakfast noted for its hospitable hosts and pleasant rooms. It is conveniently located near downtown Gatlinburg. The lodge offers a variety of luxurious accommodations, each with special features and services. The exquisite breakfast spread includes homemade goodies, and guests can unwind in the outdoor hot tub or front of the toasty fireplace.

**3. Eight Gables** Inn is a charming bed and breakfast well known for its scenic beauty and pleasant attitude. It is located in a peaceful area close to the Great Smoky Mountains National Park. The inn offers tastefully furnished rooms, some of which have private balconies with breathtaking mountain views. A delicious breakfast is offered to guests in the dining area or on the balcony. For those who love the outdoors, the inn's serene gardens and convenient location near hiking trails make it the perfect getaway.

**4. The Blue Mountain** Mist Country Inn offers a tranquil and restful retreat just minutes from Gatlinburg's attractions, and it is surrounded by rolling hills and lovely gardens. The inn offers inviting rooms and private cottages, each of which is individually designed with antique furniture and contemporary conveniences. Enjoy a delicious country breakfast, cool off in the outdoor pool, or relax with a treatment in the on-site spa while staying at the property. A home-away-from-home atmosphere is created by the inn's gracious Southern hospitality.

**5. Foxtrot Bed & Breakfast: Foxtrot** Bed and Breakfast offers a private getaway with stunning views of the Smoky Mountains, hidden away on a mountainside. The inn offers opulent rooms with whirlpool tubs, comfortable fireplaces, and private balconies. A luxurious gourmet breakfast is offered to guests in the dining area or on the patio. A romantic break is made possible by the tranquil environment and attentive care of Foxtrot Bed & Breakfast.

**6. Buckhorn Inn** is a historic bed and breakfast that radiates elegance and peace. It is only a short distance from the heart of Gatlinburg. Each of the comfortable rooms and cottages at the inn is equipped with antiques and contemporary conveniences. After a hearty breakfast, guests can explore the inn's exquisitely designed gardens or unwind on the wraparound porch. A memorable stay is produced by the tranquil setting and gracious welcome of Buckhorn Inn.

**7. A Mountain Rose Bed and Breakfast:** A Mountain Rose Bed and Breakfast offers a tranquil and romantic vacation and is located in a quiet area close to the Great Smoky Mountains National Park. The inn offers tastefully decorated rooms with opulent extras like fireplaces and whirlpool tubs. Each morning, guests can savor a lavish breakfast, unwind on the balcony, or explore the area's hiking trails. A Mountain Rose Bed and Breakfasts attentiveness to detail and individualized service guarantee a pleasurable stay.

## 4. Campgrounds and RV resorts

Gatlinburg offers something to offer any outdoor enthusiast, from picturesque campgrounds tucked away in the woods to well-equipped RV parks with contemporary amenities. To help guests plan their trip,

I'll give you a thorough description of a few well-known campgrounds and RV parks in Gatlinburg .

**1. The Smoky Bear Campground & RV Park** offers a convenient and beautiful camping experience and is only a short distance from the heart of Gatlinburg. The campsite offers roomy tent and RV camping spots, many of which are shaded and encircled by trees. There are complete connections, spotless facilities, hot showers, a laundry area, a pool, and a camp store among the amenities. Smoky Bear is a well-liked option because of its closeness to the Great Smoky Mountains National Park and the attractions of Gatlinburg.

**2. Twin Creek RV Resort** is a charming and luxurious RV park close to Gatlinburg, Tennessee, located along the Little Pigeon River. Large RV sites with full connections, picnic tables, and fire rings are available at the property. A hot tub, a pool, a clubhouse, a health center, and a game room are a few of the amenities. Outdoor enthusiasts will appreciate Twin Creek's tranquil environment and proximity to hiking and fishing destinations.

**3. Greenbrier Campground**: Located in the Great Smoky Mountains' luxuriant woodlands, Greenbrier Campground offers peaceful camping amid the great outdoors. Some of the tent and RV campsites at the park are situated along the lovely Greenbrier Creek. Hot showers, spotless facilities, a camp store, and a playground are available to campers. Greenbrier Campground is a well-liked option for outdoor enthusiasts due to its proximity to hiking trails and tranquil atmosphere.

**4. The Great Smoky Mountains** National Park's Cades Cove Campground, which offers a rustic camping experience with access to a variety of wildlife and beautiful landscapes, is situated right in the middle of the park. There are tent sites and RV sites in the campsite, some of which are first-come, first served. Restrooms, water fountains, and picnic tables are amenities. Campers may enjoy the historic Cades Cove loop and a variety of hiking trails thanks to Cades Cove's ideal position within the national park.

**5. Up the Creek RV Camp** provides a tranquil and enjoyable camping experience. It is located in a quiet valley close to Gatlinburg. The campground offers pull-through and back-in RV campsites with full hookups. A camp store, spotless facilities, hot showers, a laundry room, a swimming pool, and a playground are available as amenities. Up the Creek is a well-liked option for nature enthusiasts due to its serene surroundings and proximity to hiking trails and fishing streams.

**6. The Camp LeConte Luxury** Outdoor Resort offers a distinctive glamping experience close to Gatlinburg by fusing the conveniences of a resort with the fun of camping. Safari tents, treehouses, and RV sites are just a few of the resort's lodging choices. Comfortable bedrooms, private baths, fully functional kitchens, and outdoor fire pits are among the amenities available to visitors. Camp LeConte is a great option for people looking for a premium camping experience due to its high-end amenities and proximity to outdoor activities.

# Chapter 4: Gatlinburg's Currency

## 1. Gatlinburg Dollar

Tennessee's Great Smoky Mountains are home to the popular tourist attraction of Gatlinburg, recognized for its scenic beauty, outdoor recreation, and energetic lifestyle. Although Gatlinburg lacks its currency, the United States dollar (USD), which is widely accepted in the region, serves as the town's official unit of exchange.

Gatlinburg utilizes the USD as its official currency because it is a part of the US. All financial transactions in Gatlinburg are conducted using the dollar, which is the most extensively used and recognized currency in the entire world. In the town, both visitors and locals can use the USD to make purchases, pay for services, and carry out any other financial operations.

The Federal Reserve System, the country's central banking system, is in charge of issuing the USD. Coins (pennies, nickels, dimes, and quarters) and banknotes (one dollar, five dollars, ten dollars, twenty dollars, fifty dollars, and one hundred dollars) are both available in a variety of denominations. Individuals can use these currencies for both little and large transactions.

There are many banks and currency exchange offices in Gatlinburg where foreign currencies can be converted into US dollars. This makes it simple for visitors from other countries to convert their local currency into US dollars for usage while they are there. Depending on market conditions and variables affecting the world economy, exchange rates between various currencies and the USD may change.

Gatlinburg is a popular tourist destination with a thriving economy and a wide variety of businesses that serve the requirements of travelers. The town is home to a wide variety of enterprises, including dining establishments, lodging facilities, gift stores, outdoor activity providers, and entertainment venues. These establishments often accept cash, credit cards, and debit cards, making it simple for tourists to take advantage of Gatlinburg without having to worry about money-related concerns.

Gatlinburg has seen a rise in the usage of electronic payment methods like credit cards, which is consistent with the general trend in the United States and around the world. Major credit cards, including Visa, Mastercard, American Express, and Discover, are accepted by the majority of Gatlinburg businesses.

## 2. Where to Find Money Exchange

Gatlinburg offers numerous opportunities for guests to convert their local currency into United States dollars (USD) as it is a well-known vacation destination. Despite the lack of specialized currency exchange facilities in the area, visitors can obtain currency exchange services at several businesses. In Gatlinburg, you have the following choices for money exchange:

**1. Banks and other financial institutions:** There are branches of well-known banks in Gatlinburg, including

Bank of America, Wells Fargo, and BB&T. For their clients, these institutions frequently provide currency exchange services. These banks welcome visitors who want to learn more about their rules and costs related to currency exchange. It's a good idea to call your bank in advance to see if there are any partnerships or branches there.

**2. Currency Exchange Bureaus:** There may be currency exchange bureaus in some of the bigger Gatlinburg-area communities, such as Knoxville. Currency exchange facilities are available in the airport terminals of Knoxville's McGhee Tyson Airport for travelers arriving by plane. Larger hotels in Gatlinburg might also provide their visitors with currency exchange facilities. It is advised to get in touch with your hotel in advance to ask about this service.

**3. Online Currency Exchange**: Websites that offer currency exchange services online give customers a practical choice. With the help of these sites, you can convert your local currency into US dollars online and either have the money delivered to your home or pick it up in person nearby. Before making a purchase, make sure to look up trustworthy online currency conversion providers and compare exchange rates and fees.

**4. ATMs**: Gatlinburg is home to many easily accessible ATMs. These ATMs allow visitors to make USD cash withdrawals using their local debit or credit cards from other countries. It's crucial to be informed of any additional costs and exchange rate surcharges levied by your home bank. Make that your card can be used for international withdrawals by contacting your bank, and asking about any fees associated with international transactions.

**5. Major credit cards** are accepted by the majority of Gatlinburg businesses, including hotels, restaurants, and shops. A handy method of payment is via credit card, as the transaction will be automatically converted to US dollars depending on the current exchange rate. To ensure uninterrupted use and to learn about any potential international transaction fees, it is advised to let your credit card company know about your vacation intentions.

It's crucial to take current exchange rates and associated costs into account when exchanging money. Exchange rates may differ between service providers, so it is a good idea to compare prices to make sure you get a good conversion.

## 3. Budgeting & Money

To ensure a smooth and pleasurable trip, it's crucial to budget sensibly and manage your money when visiting Gatlinburg as a visitor. Here are some practical advice and ideas for managing your finances and creating a budget in Gatlinburg:

**1. Currency:** The United States dollar (USD) is the accepted form of payment in Gatlinburg. It's a good idea to convert your home currency to US dollars before your travel. You can accomplish this at banks, currency exchange bureaus, or internet exchange services. Learn about the current exchange rates and any associated costs before you exchange any money.

**2. Establishing a Budget**: Set a reasonable spending limit for your trip to Gatlinburg. Take into account all the key costs, including lodging, travel, food, attractions, and mementos. Establishing a budget requires doing some research on the typical prices for these things in Gatlinburg. Setting up some extra money for unforeseen costs or emergencies is usually a good idea.

**3. Gatlinburg provides a selection of lodging choices, including hotels, motels, cabins, and vacation rentals.** The costs vary according to the area, the extras, and the season of the year. When choosing a place to stay, keep in mind your preferences and spending limit. You should also account for any supplemental expenses like taxes and resort fees.

**4. Transportation: If** you're flying to Gatlinburg, compare flight costs and select the flight that is the most affordable. When you arrive in Gatlinburg, think about using the Gatlinburg Trolley, which has reasonable fares and easy routes throughout the town. Exploring the downtown area on foot is another option.

**5. Dining: Gatlinburg** offers a variety of dining alternatives for all price ranges. You can choose from premium restaurants to affordable places, depending on your interests. Consider eating at neighborhood diners, and cafes, or purchasing food from food trucks to save money. Additionally, some lodgings have free breakfasts, which might help you start the day on a tight budget.

6. Gatlinburg provides a wide range of sights to see and things to do, including hiking trails, museums, amusement parks, and beautiful drives. Prioritize these attractions based on your preferences and spending power after doing some advanced research on the costs involved. To get the most out of your money, look for discounted tickets, combo deals, or free attractions.

**7. Shopping and souvenirs:** Gatlinburg is renowned for its distinctive local crafts and souvenir shops. Set a spending limit for memento purchases and adhere to it.

Explore other retailers to compare costs and hunt for offers or discounts. Keep in mind that occasionally, local markets or artisan festivals are the finest places to find mementos.

**8. Payment Options:** Credit and debit cards are very often used in Gatlinburg, but cash is also accepted everywhere. Bring a variety of payment options with you for ease and security. To prevent any problems with card usage, inform your bank or credit card provider of your vacation plans. Keep an eye on your expenditures and frequently check the balances in your accounts.

**9. offers & Discounts:** Take advantage of any offers, coupons, or discounts provided by local tourism websites, restaurants, and attractions. For the most recent promos, check internet resources, neighborhood guides, or visitor centers. This can enable you to save money while still taking advantage of Gatlinburg's top attractions.

**10. Use these additional suggestions** to save money while visiting Gatlinburg:

- Look for coupons or other special offers for restaurants and activities.

- If you have access to a kitchenette or outdoor grilling equipment, cook part of your meals.

- Benefit from free activities and sights, such as parks, hiking trails, and stunning vistas.

- To stay hydrated, use water fountains or refillable water bottles rather than buying bottled water.

**11. Emergencies and contingencies**: It's a good idea to keep some extra cash on hand or a backup means of payment in case of emergencies or if you run into places that only accept cash. It is also advised to have travel insurance to pay for any unplanned costs or emergencies while traveling.

# Chapter 5: Gatlinburg Language

## 1. Gatlinburg English

English is widely used throughout the United States, including Gatlinburg, Tennessee. English is the official language of the nation, and both locals and tourists in Gatlinburg are fluent in it. The majority of the local population speaks English fluently, including service providers, hotel personnel, and company owners.

Gatlinburg is a popular tourist destination that draws tourists from all over the world, therefore it's usual to hear people speaking many languages there. However, English continues to be the most common language used for communication in most contexts, such as dealings with locals, tourist services, and official institutions.

English-speaking guests may easily navigate the town and receive necessary services in Gatlinburg because many businesses here have signage, menus, information boards, and other printed items in English. English is used to provide efficient communication and to make traveling easier for visitors.

Even though English is the dominant language, you could run into people who speak different languages. Gatlinburg's tourism sector employs a broad workforce, making it easier to locate multilingual staff members who can assist tourists in languages like Spanish, French, German, or other widely spoken languages.

Additionally, in well-known tourist locations, you might find multilingual tourist information centers or translation services. These services are designed to meet the demands of foreign visitors and guarantee their comfort and enjoyment while they are in Gatlinburg.

Carrying translation software or a pocket phrasebook can be useful if you are not a native English speaker or feel more comfortable speaking a language other than English to assist in basic conversation. Even though English is commonly spoken, making an effort to acquire a few basic English phrases will improve your trip and interactions with locals.

Gatlinburg values the diversity of culture and welcomes guests from all walks of life. The majority of the people in the area are kind and understanding, eager to help, and engage in conversation with visitors to ensure they have a good day. If you run into any language issues or require assistance while visiting Gatlinburg, don't be afraid to ask for assistance or clarification.

## 2. language Expressions

Knowing some basic English idioms to utilize in various contexts can be helpful when traveling to Gatlinburg as a visitor. The following words and phrases may come in handy while you're here:

**1. Greetings and Foundational Words:**
"Hello" or "Hi" is used as a standard salutation.
- "Good morning/afternoon/evening" - A greeting used to indicate the time of day.

-A standard greeting and conversation opener is "How are you?"

-"Thank you" is a phrase used to show appreciation.

- "You're welcome" is the reply to "Thank you."

- "Excuse me" - Used to draw attention to oneself or to express regret.

- "I'm sorry" - A phrase used to express regret for any inconvenience or error.

**2. Requesting Information**

"Can you help me, please?" is a phrase used to request assistance.

- "Where is...?" - To ask where a certain site or tourist attraction is.

- "How do I get to...?" - Requesting a specific location's directions.

- "What time does...open/close?" - When requesting information about a location's business hours.

# Chapter 6: Gatlinburg's Attractions

## 1. Great Smoky Mountains National Park

Great Smoky Mountains National Park is a true gem of unspoiled beauty and a popular travel destination for people from all over the world. It is close to Gatlinburg, Tennessee. This magnificent national park, which covers an area of more than 800 square miles, is well-known for its gorgeous scenery, varied animals, and rich cultural legacy. The Great Smoky Mountains National Park offers a wealth of experiences that will leave you in amazement, whether you're an outdoor enthusiast, a nature lover, or someone looking for peace.

The Great Smoky Mountains National Park is known for its magnificent mountain ranges, which provide the setting for a wide variety of excursions. Over 100 peaks in the park are higher than 5,000 feet, including the well-known Clingmans Dome, which is the highest point in Tennessee. With a variety of trails suitable for hikers of all levels, backpackers, and photographers may enjoy these gorgeous mountains as a playground. There is a path for everyone to explore and enjoy, from easy multi-day hikes through the untamed backcountry to strolls along the picturesque roadways.

The park is a haven for a remarkable variety of plant and animal species, making it a haven for nature photographers and wildlife aficionados. Black bears, white-tailed deer, elk, wild turkeys, and a wide variety of smaller creatures and birds may be seen as you walk the park's paths. Over 1,500 types of flowering plants, including the recognizable flame azaleas and delicate trilliums, are supported by the park's various ecosystems. While the beautiful autumn foliage covers the scene in shades of red, orange, and gold, the springtime delivers a riot of color as the mountains are covered with blooming wildflowers. Every time you visit the park, you can enjoy a different show that changes with the seasons.

The Great Smoky Mountains National Park also has a rich historical and cultural history in addition to its natural beauty. Many log homes, barns, and churches that were formerly a part of thriving Appalachian mountain towns are maintained within the park. With its well-preserved old houses and charming loop road, Cades Cove, a gorgeous valley inside the park, offers a glimpse into the area's past and lets tourists travel back in time. The park also holds a variety of cultural activities, such as performances of traditional music and exhibitions of traditional crafts, giving visitors a chance to become immersed in the region's rich past.

The Great Smoky Mountains National Park provides a variety of services and amenities to improve the visitor experience. The Sugarlands Visitor Center in the vicinity of Gatlinburg is a great place to start because it offers details on the park's attractions, trail maps, and educational exhibits. In the park, there are many campgrounds and picnic places that let tourists unwind in the great outdoors while also spending quality time with family and friends. Additionally, anglers can cast their lines into the park's rivers and streams, which are renowned for having large concentrations of trout.

## 2. Ober Gatlinburg

Gatlinburg, Tennessee's Ober Gatlinburg is a top travel destination for tourists looking for a distinctive combination of outdoor adventure, family-friendly entertainment, and breathtaking mountain panoramas. It is located in the heart of the Great Smoky Mountains. Ober Gatlinburg, perched atop Mount Harrison, has a wide range of activities and attractions that appeal to people of all ages and interests, guaranteeing each guest an outstanding experience.

One of Ober Gatlinburg's features is its world-famous ski resort, which draws fans of winter sports from all over. Visitors can enjoy the excitement of sliding down snowy hills in inflatable tubes or carve their way through powdery slopes on nine ski trails that range from beginner to advanced levels. Modern snowmaking technology at the resort guarantees the best skiing conditions all winter long. The well-maintained slopes and qualified instructors at Ober Gatlinburg make it a great location for winter sports fans, regardless of whether you are an experienced skier or a beginner eager to learn.

Ober Gatlinburg has a range of additional outdoor activities year-round in addition to skiing and snowboarding. The resort morphs into a hotspot of outdoor adventure during the warmer months, offering pursuits like beautiful chairlift rides, alpine slides, and a mountain coaster. The Aerial Tramway, a well-liked attraction, takes guests from downtown Gatlinburg to the mountainside while offering spectacular panoramic vistas and a different viewpoint of the surrounding Smoky Mountains.

Ober Gatlinburg is also home to the Wildlife Encounter, where guests may get up-close views of local Appalachian species. The Wildlife Encounter offers an educational and participatory experience that creates a deeper understanding of the area's natural history, with everything from playful river otters to majestic birds of prey. The resort also provides guided hiking excursions that let guests explore the lovely paths and learn about the varied flora and animals of the Great Smoky Mountains.

Ober Gatlinburg offers a variety of family-friendly attractions and entertainment choices in addition to outdoor pursuits. The amusement park offers limitless entertainment for both kids and adults with its carousel, mini golf course, maze, and water raft ride. Visitors to the resort can take advantage of the indoor ice rink, test their reflexes in the arcade, or enjoy dining and shopping in the Alpine Village, which has a charming Bavarian-inspired ambiance.

Additionally, Ober Gatlinburg provides a range of eating alternatives to suit all tastes. Visitors can have a wonderful dinner while admiring the breathtaking views of the nearby mountains at any number of fine dining establishments, from upmarket restaurants with panoramic views to intimate cafes providing hearty mountain fare. The restaurants in Ober Gatlinburg provide a variety of cuisines to suit a variety of tastes and preferences, whether you're craving a hefty meal of Southern barbecue, a juicy burger, or a sweet treat from the fudge shop.

Ober Gatlinburg offers a wide range of amenities and services to make sure that your trip is smooth and pleasurable. The resort provides ski, snowboard, and ice skating equipment rentals so that guests may conveniently participate in the various activities without the burden of bringing their equipment. The resort also features many lounging places and observation decks that offer opportunities for relaxation and taking in stunning mountain views.

## 3. Skylift Park in Gatlinburg:

The lovely mountain town of Gatlinburg, Tennessee, is home to the Gatlinburg SkyLift Park, a must-see location for tourists seeking breathtaking scenery, outdoor adventure, and a unique experience in the heart of the Great Smoky Mountains. The park, which is perched atop Crockett Mountain, provides both people and families wishing to take in the area's natural beauty with a variety of attractions and activities.

The renowned SkyLift, a picturesque chairlift that takes passengers to the summit while offering breathtaking panoramic views along the way, is the focal point of Gatlinburg SkyLift Park. The splendor of the Great Smoky Mountains unfolds before your eyes as you climb through the dense forests and over the falling streams. A large observation deck with unobstructed views of the surrounding mountains, valleys, and the quaint town of Gatlinburg nestling below awaits you once you reach the summit. At sunrise and sunset, when the sky is painted with vivid hues, the stunning sights are especially mesmerizing and genuinely amazing.

The park offers a range of attractions and activities in addition to the SkyLift to cater to a variety of interests. The SkyBridge is the longest pedestrian suspension bridge in North America and one of the park's most well-liked attractions. The SkyBridge offers unmatched vistas of the Smoky Mountains by allowing guests to feel as though they are strolling amid the treetops thanks to its translucent floor panels. The thrilling experience of crossing the bridge shouldn't be missed.

The Gatlinburg SkyDeck, which includes a demanding yet thrilling series of interactive elements, including a glass-bottomed viewing point and an exhilarating spiral staircase that leads to a bird's-eye view of the park, is available at Gatlinburg SkyLift Park for thrill-seekers. With educational signage emphasizing the area's ecology, fauna, and history, the SkyTrail offers a chance to explore the mountain's natural splendor at your speed.

The park offers relaxing lounging places and picnic locations where visitors may unwind and take in the tranquil surroundings for those looking for a more leisurely experience. You can relax with a snack or peruse a selection of one-of-a-kind gifts and regional crafts at the Gatlinburg SkyCenter, a hilltop café and gift shop.

In addition to hosting regular events all year long, Gatlinburg SkyLift Park also celebrates holidays and other special occasions. Every visit to the park is sure to be a memorable one because there is always something going on, from holiday-themed festivals to live music performances and art exhibits.

The park offers practical amenities and services to improve the visiting experience. Visitors can easily combine their visit to the park with their investigation of the neighborhood because parking facilities are provided and the park is accessible from downtown Gatlinburg. The park also provides a variety of ticket choices, including reduced prices for kids and families, making it a reachable and inexpensive vacation spot for everyone.

In addition to providing spectacular views and exhilarating attractions, Gatlinburg SkyLift Park also acts as a starting point for exploring the Great Smoky

Mountains National Park's natural beauties. Indulge in the beauty of the historic mountains, flowing waterfalls, and varied fauna that make the region so special as you ride the SkyLift down the mountain and continue your experience by exploring the hiking trails and beautiful drives of the national park.

## 4. Smokies' version of Ripley's Aquarium:

In the charming Tennessee town of Gatlinburg, there is a top-notch attraction called Ripley's Aquarium of the Smokies that transports guests to an enthralling underwater realm. The aquarium, one of the most well-liked tourist attractions in the Smoky Mountains, gives visitors of all ages a fantastic opportunity to observe aquatic life from a variety of settings throughout the world.

You are welcomed by a wide variety of exhibits and interactive displays that highlight the wonders of the ocean when you enter Ripley's Aquarium of the

Smokies. More than 10,000 unusual sea animals from more than 350 species can be found at the aquarium. Every nook of the aquarium offers a new and interesting facet of marine life, from the vivid fish and fragile coral reefs of the Tropical Rainforest exhibit to the hypnotic jellyfish in the Ocean Realm display.

The Penguin Playhouse, a habitat that resembles the Antarctic environment and is home to a comical colony of cute penguins, is one of the aquarium's attractions. This captivating and immersive experience allows visitors to watch these beautiful birds as they swim, slide, and interact with their surroundings. With the help of the Penguin Encounter program, visitors can get even closer to a penguin and learn more about its habits and conservation activities.

Shark Lagoon is just one of the unique experiences that Ripley's Aquarium of the Smokies has to offer thrill-seekers. Visitors can pass through a translucent tunnel as sharks, including sawfish and sand tiger sharks, gracefully swim above them. You may see these magnificent predators up close and get a better appreciation of how important they are to marine ecology through this thrilling encounter.

The Coral Reef, which displays the vivid hues and intricate patterns of coral formations, is another intriguing exhibit. Here, tourists can be astounded by the variety of marine life, including vibrant reef fish, eels, and even sea turtles, that live in these sensitive habitats. Educational exhibits offer details on the significance of coral conservation and the difficulties facing these vulnerable areas.

Additionally, a variety of interactive games and programs are available at Ripley's Aquarium of the Smokies to immerse guests in learning. There are opportunities to better your understanding of marine life and the initiatives made to protect and maintain our oceans, from touch tanks where you may gently engage with rays and horseshoe crabs to behind-the-scenes tours that offer a peek into the aquarium's inner workings.

The aquarium hosts a range of unique events and shows all year long in addition to its fascinating exhibits. These occasions could be dive shows, where knowledgeable commentary is provided while expert divers engage with marine life or instructional talks that concentrate on certain facets of marine biology. The aquarium often hosts fun and instructive events that draw people back time and time again.

Ripley's Aquarium of the Smokies offers practical conveniences and services to guarantee a smooth and pleasurable stay. Visitors can eat while taking in panoramic views of the exhibits at the facility's dining establishments. Additionally, there are gift stores where you may pick up a variety of marine-themed trinkets to remember your visit to the aquarium.

Families can take advantage of the aquarium's educational and entertaining atmosphere for kids. The aquarium encourages awe and curiosity about the aquatic environment through interactive displays, educational events, and play spaces made especially for children.

Families may make enduring memories there while also learning about the beauty and diversity of our waters.

## 5. Space Needle in Gatlinburg:

Visitors seeking panoramic vistas, family-friendly activities, and a distinctive viewpoint of the Great Smoky Mountains should not miss the Gatlinburg Space Needle, a famous landmark located in the center of downtown Gatlinburg, Tennessee. The Space Needle, which soars to a height of 407 feet, provides an exhilarating and immersive experience that captures the spirit of the Smoky Mountains unlike anything else.

Visitors are welcomed by a lively complex at the base of the Gatlinburg Space Needle, which is home to a variety of attractions and activities. Of course, the elevator journey that quickly takes you to the observation deck at the top of the Needle is the primary feature. Ascending with anticipation, you are rewarded with stunning

360-degree views of the surrounding mountains, valleys, and the quaint town of Gatlinburg below once you emerge onto the deck.

Visitors can take in the natural splendor of the Great Smoky Mountains National Park, the most visited national park in the country, from the observation deck. Sweeping views provide a sight of the park's lush forests, imposing peaks, and tumbling waterfalls, inspiring awe and respect for the magnificence of nature. When the sky is ablaze with brilliant colors at sunrise or sunset, creating a picture-perfect background for your visit, the vistas are especially mesmerizing.

The Space Needle provides high-powered viewfinders that let you zoom in and examine particular points of interest in more detail to improve the experience. These viewfinders offer an engaging and educational component to your stay, deepening your comprehension of the area's geography and natural beauty. They can be used to identify distant mountain peaks or spot sites in Gatlinburg.

The Gatlinburg Space Needle complex includes additional attractions that appeal to a variety of interests in addition to stunning views. At the foot of the Space Needle, the Iris Theater hosts live performances of everything from musical productions to magic shows. You may unwind and take in some top-notch entertainment at this charming and interesting location while you're there.

The Space Needle also has the Arcadia amusement complex, which has a variety of interactive games and activities, for those looking for a little excitement. Everyone may enjoy everything from vintage arcade games to cutting-edge virtual reality experiences. Visitors may put their abilities to the test, compete with friends and family, and make lifelong memories at this fun family activity.

The Gatlinburg Space Needle complex provides a range of dining establishments and gift shops so you may further remember your trip there. You can have a meal or indulge in sweet delights while admiring the breathtaking views at every type of restaurant, from casual eateries that serve delectable snacks and refreshments to expensive diners that offer panoramic views of the nearby mountains. You can bring a bit of the Gatlinburg experience home with you by purchasing one-of-a-kind souvenirs, regional crafts, and presents from the souvenir stores.

Accessibility and convenience are top priorities at the Gatlinburg Space Needle facility. It is simple for guests to access the attraction and explore the nearby downtown area because there is plenty of parking accessible. You may easily combine your visit with your tour of Gatlinburg's colorful ambiance because of the complex's strategic proximity to other well-liked attractions, stores, and restaurants.

## 6. Hollywood star automobile museum

Intriguing and engaging, the Hollywood Star Cars Museum in Gatlinburg, Tennessee, lets visitors get up close and personal with famous cars from the entertainment industry. This distinctive museum, which is situated right in the middle of downtown Gatlinburg, features an impressive collection of vehicles that have been on film, making it a must-see destination for both movie fans and auto enthusiasts.

You are immediately thrust into a world of Hollywood glitz and cinematic history as soon as you enter the Hollywood Star Cars Museum. The museum is home to an extraordinary collection of automobiles that have appeared prominently in adored movies and television programs. Every exhibit, from well-known movie automobiles to vehicles owned by celebrities, has a tale to tell and provides a window into the enchantment of the entertainment business.

The opportunity to view renowned vehicles from vintage films is one of the museum's highlights. Whether it's the familiar Batmobile from the "Batman" series, the iconic DeLorean time machine from "Back to the Future," or the Ecto-1 from Ghostbusters, you may marvel at these recognizable vehicles and relive the memorable scenes from your favorite movies. Visitors can see the workmanship and artistry that went into the design of these vehicles thanks to the meticulous attention to detail in their restoration and preservation.

The Hollywood Star Cars Museum includes vehicles from current blockbusters and well-liked TV shows in addition to vintage automobiles. The "Fast and Furious" vehicles, the swanky automobiles from the "James Bond" films, or even the recognizable General Lee from "Dukes of Hazzard" could come across your path. As you move around the museum, you'll find yourself immersed in a fantastical world where the lines between fact and fiction are blurred and the automobiles take on the significance of larger-than-life representations of the people and events they represent.

The museum provides a lot of knowledge and behind-the-scenes insights in addition to the opportunity to view these amazing automobiles. The automobiles, their history, and their position in the entertainment business are all covered in interesting detail by interactive exhibitions, educational plaques, and experienced staff members. You'll get a deeper understanding of the craft of filmmaking and the crucial role that vehicles play in bringing tales to life on the big screen from the technical details to the anecdotes and facts.

The Hollywood Star Cars Museum offers photo opportunities with a few vehicles to help make your trip even more memorable. Imagine taking pictures next to the Jeep from "Jurassic Park" or driving the legendary "Scooby-Doo" Mystery Machine. With the help of these photo ops, you may immortalize your trip to the museum and capture a moment of Hollywood magic.

The museum is committed to giving visitors an engaging experience that goes beyond the actual displays. There is a gift store at the Hollywood Star Cars Museum where you may look through a variety of movie-related memorabilia, collectibles, and trinkets. There is something for every fan to take home and treasure as a souvenir of their visit, ranging from T-shirts and posters to model vehicles and movie memorabilia.

The Hollywood Star Cars Museum also places a high priority on convenience and accessibility. The museum is conveniently situated in the heart of Gatlinburg, making it accessible to those touring the neighborhood. Additionally, there are many parking lots close by, guaranteeing a hassle-free trip.

The Hollywood Star Cars Museum in Gatlinburg, Tennessee, is a fascinating place that blends the thrill of iconic movie vehicles with a celebration of cinematic history, to sum up. This distinctive museum provides an engaging and instructive experience for visitors of all ages, featuring vintage automobiles and contemporary icons. A trip to the Hollywood Star Cars Museum promises to be an exciting excursion into the world of Hollywood glitz and fantasy.

## 7. Gatlinburg's artistic community:

A haven for imagination, skill, and artistic expression, the Gatlinburg Arts and Crafts Community is situated just beyond the busy downtown area of Gatlinburg, Tennessee. This distinctive village, the largest collection of independent artists in North America, spans an astounding 8-mile loop road and provides tourists with an immersive and educational experience in the field of arts and crafts.

You'll be met by a lively and warm ambiance as soon as you enter the Gatlinburg Arts and Crafts Community. Over 100 talented craftspeople and artists who represent a variety of fields and artistic styles live in the neighborhood. The local art scene is represented by a variety of artists in the community, including painters, potters, woodworkers, and weavers.

The chance to observe the creative process directly is one of the pleasures of exploring the neighborhood. Many artisans invite people to view them as they painstakingly construct their creations in their open-air studios and workshops. This personal exchange forges a special bond between the artist and the spectators and sheds light on the methods, sources of inspiration, and narratives that go into each work of art.

You'll come across a rich tapestry of artistic materials and styles as you explore the Gatlinburg Arts and Crafts Community. The astonishing variety of artwork on show at galleries and studios includes everything from classic paintings of mountain vistas and fauna to modern sculptures and avant-garde installations. You're sure to uncover works that capture your imagination and appeal to your particular taste, whether you're an experienced art collector or simply appreciate artistic expression.

Along with visual arts, the area is well known for its fine handiwork and classic Appalachian crafts. Unique pottery, complex textiles, beautiful stained glass, and expertly created wooden furniture are among the specialties of local artisans. Each item bears traces of the region's rich cultural heritage and workmanship, which attests to the artists' talent and commitment.

The Gatlinburg Arts and Crafts Community gives visitors the ability to participate in practical experiences in addition to appreciating and purchasing art. For individuals willing to develop new abilities or discover their artistic potential, workshops, and programs are offered. These participatory programs, which range from pottery throwing to painting lessons, give participants a creative and informative outlet and let them take home their handcrafted treasures and memories.

It's not just about the art when you explore the area; you can also get a taste of the endearing Appalachian tradition. You can find charming stores and inviting cafés that highlight regional cuisines and classic Appalachian cuisine around circle road. The gastronomic choices reflect the friendly friendliness and rich culinary traditions of the area, with everything from homemade fudge and freshly baked delicacies to hearty cuisine inspired by the mountains.

A crucial component of the Gatlinburg Arts and Crafts Community is convenience and accessibility. There is plenty of parking along the circular road, which is simple to manage. The neighborhood offers a laid-back and friendly atmosphere for tourists to explore at their own pace whether they decide to drive the circle road or take a stroll.

A trip to the Gatlinburg Arts and Crafts Community is more than just a shopping excursion; it's also a celebration of the locals' creativity, skill, and artistic spirit. It's a chance to interact with artists, find out about their backgrounds and sources of inspiration, and bring a piece of Gatlinburg's thriving and diverse art scene home. Whether you're an avid art collector, an inquisitive traveler, or just looking for a special and genuine experience, a trip to the Gatlinburg Arts and Crafts Community is guaranteed to spark your imagination and give you a newfound understanding of the value of handcrafted artwork.

## 8. A mountain coaster in Gatlinburg:

Visitors can go on a remarkable trip on the exhilarating and adrenaline-pumping Gatlinburg Mountain Coaster, which is located in the picturesque mountains of Gatlinburg, Tennessee. Visitors of all ages will have an incredible experience on this one-of-a-kind coaster, which blends the thrill of a roller coaster with the scenic grandeur of the Smoky Mountains.

You'll be seated in a cozy single or double-rider sled-like cart as you board the Gatlinburg Mountain Coaster. You will be sent twisting and turning along the mountainside as the roller coaster makes its way through the beautiful countryside. The ride's design ensures an exhilarating experience while keeping safety and control by achieving the ideal combination of speed, bends, and drops.

The Gatlinburg Mountain Coaster's adaptability and modification are two of its most noteworthy qualities. The ability to choose one's speed gives riders the opportunity for a unique experience. The coaster lets you customize the ride to your comfort level and preferences, whether you like a leisurely cruise through the mountains while taking in the gorgeous view, or an adrenaline-fueled adventure while speeding through the twists and turns.

You'll be treated to breathtaking views of the surrounding Smoky Mountains as you travel the coaster's track. Your experience will take place against a completely immersive and breathtaking backdrop of rich foliage, majestic peaks, and expansive views. The Gatlinburg Mountain Coaster is a singular and unforgettable experience that perfectly embodies the spirit of the Great Smoky Mountains thanks to its blend of heart-pounding exhilaration and unmatched natural beauty.

Visitors can experience the excitement of the ride at any time of year because the coaster runs all year round. As you speed through the turns during the warmer months, you may feel the cooling mountain breeze. You can fully appreciate the splendor of the autumn season when the leaves are changing color, which creates a lovely backdrop in the fall. The coaster delivers a one-of-a-kind experience year-round as you soar through landscapes blanketed in snow, turning your journey into a winter wonderland.

All riders will experience safety and enjoyment on the Gatlinburg Mountain Coaster. Each guest receives a thorough safety briefing before riding, and the coaster follows rigorous operational and maintenance guidelines. You can feel comfortable as you move around the tracks thanks to the safety features and snug belts that are included in the carts.

The Gatlinburg Mountain Coaster provides customers with comfortable conveniences and services in addition to the thrill of the ride itself. The attraction often has a ticket office or visitor center where you can buy tickets, get more information about the experience, and get any other help you might need. You might also have access to concessions or snack stands so you can refuel and rejuvenate following your journey.

The Gatlinburg Mountain Coaster is conveniently situated close to other well-liked attractions, stores, and dining establishments. This makes it simple to include a ride on the coaster into your exploration of the area as a whole, leading to a satisfying and unique holiday.

## 9. Fun on Gatlin's Smoky Mountain:

Gatlin's Smoky Mountain Fun, a bustling and varied entertainment complex offering guests a wide selection of activities, attractions, and family-friendly fun, is situated in the center of Gatlinburg, Tennessee. Gatlin's Smoky Mountain Fun offers an immersive and unforgettable experience for visitors of all ages, with everything from exhilarating rides and interactive activities to live entertainment and delectable culinary selections.

The variety of thrilling rides at Gatlin's Smoky Mountain Fun is one of its key attractions. There is something for everyone, regardless of your preference for an exhilarating encounter or a more relaxed one. In addition to exhilarating roller coasters that will leave you gasping for air, the complex has go-kart tracks where you can try your racing prowess, bumper cars for some friendly competition, and more. These rides are ideal for thrill-seekers and those looking for a more laid-back journey since they provide just the right amount of fun and excitement.

Gatlin's Smoky Mountain Fun offers a variety of interactive games and activities in addition to its exhilarating rides. There are countless chances for enjoyment and friendly rivalry, from vintage arcade games to cutting-edge virtual reality experiences. Visitors can compete with one another and their friends to win prizes, test their abilities in a variety of games, and make treasured memories of happy times.

Another important component of Gatlin's Smoky Mountain Fun is live entertainment. The complex frequently organizes shows by accomplished musicians, comedians, and magicians, allowing guests to unwind, relax, and take in a live performance. These performances, which range from musical acts to humorous routines, offer another level of excitement and enjoyment to your visit, giving the whole family a well-rounded experience.

Gatlin's Smoky Mountain Fun features a variety of dining alternatives for you. The complex is home to many eateries and snack stalls that provide a variety of mouthwatering and filling options. There is food to fulfill every appetite, ranging from fast nibbles and traditional amusement park fare to sit-down restaurants providing delectable dinners. Take your family out to a leisurely supper or get a quick snack to fill up before continuing your excursions.

Additionally, Gatlin's Smoky Mountain Fun appreciates the value of accessibility and convenience. The complex includes plenty of parking spaces, which makes it simple for guests to access the attractions and have a good time without any worry. Additionally, Gatlin's Smoky Mountain Fun is conveniently close to other well-liked attractions, retail districts, and lodging options in Gatlinburg, making it simple to include your visit into your overall schedule and guaranteeing a smooth and delightful encounter.

The complex's devotion to safety demonstrates its dedication to client happiness. All rides and attractions are kept in good condition and are subject to routine inspections thanks to Gatlin's Smoky Mountain Fun's scrupulous adherence to safety standards and requirements. A safe and pleasurable visit is guaranteed for all visitors by trained staff members who are also on hand to offer help.

# Chapter 7: Outdoor Recreations

## 1. Paths for Nature Hikes:

Outdoor fans seeking adventure and breathtaking scenery will find nirvana in Gatlinburg, Tennessee, which is tucked away in the Great Smoky Mountains. Thanks to its vast network of beautiful paths that are suitable for hikers of all levels, Gatlinburg boasts one of the most well-liked outdoor recreation areas.

There are numerous hiking opportunities available in Gatlinburg, ranging from strolls to strenuous climbs, so there is something for everyone. You may find routes that highlight the area's gorgeous landscapes, unique flora and wildlife, and breathtaking views, whether you're an experienced hiker or a first-time traveler.

Gatlinburg has several lovely nature paths that meander through thick forests, next to bubbling streams, and across tranquil meadows for those looking for a leisurely trek. These Families and individuals wishing to immerse themselves in the peace of the Smokies will find the Gatlinburg Trail, Sugarlands Valley Nature Trail, and Fighting Creek Nature Trail to be ideal.

If you're looking for a more difficult adventure, Gatlinburg has a variety of routes that lead to stunning views and thrilling encounters. The Alum Cave Trail, which passes through unique geological formations and ends at the breathtaking Alum Cave Bluffs, is one of the most famous hikes. The Rainbow Falls Trail is another well-liked trail and is well-known for its magnificent 80-foot cascade that sparkles in the sunlight and frequently produces brilliant rainbows.

Gatlinburg acts as a starting point for those who enjoy hiking and the outdoors to access the renowned Appalachian Trail. From Georgia to Maine, this amazing long-distance track travels 2,100 miles over fourteen states. The entire trail may be hiked, but Gatlinburg offers access points for day hikes or shorter backpacking trips along this well-known route.

Gatlinburg has a variety of additional outdoor activities in addition to hiking so that guests can fully appreciate the natural marvels in the area. Fly fishers can cast their lines into the crystal-clear alpine streams in an attempt to catch trout. The abundance of fishing options in the Great Smoky Mountains National Park, which includes Gatlinburg, is well-known.

Whitewater rafting and other adrenaline-pumping activities can be found in Gatlinburg for thrill-seekers. The neighboring Pigeon River is a well-liked location for rafting excursions ideal for all skill levels because it has thrilling rapids and gorgeous scenery. Another thrilling alternative is zip-lining, which enables you to soar through the treetops and take in breathtaking panoramic vistas of the Smokies.

Camping is a great way to experience all that Gatlinburg's outdoors has to offer. You can spend tranquil nights beneath a blanket of stars at one of the many campsites and backcountry camping locations offered by the Great Smoky Mountains National Park.

Whatever outdoor activity you decide to partake in while visiting Gatlinburg, you can expect to have a wonderful time in nature. Gatlinburg is a paradise for individuals seeking outdoor discovery and a close connection with the breathtaking landscapes of the Great Smoky Mountains, offering calm nature walks, strenuous treks, thrilling water adventures, and serene camping areas.

## 2. Observing Wildlife

Gatlinburg not only has gorgeous outdoor scenery and activities, but it also has fantastic possibilities to see animals. Gatlinburg offers a habitat for a wide range of animal species because it is located within the Great Smoky Mountains National Park, one of the most biodiverse places in North America.

Wildlife that can be spotted in Gatlinburg includes black bears, white-tailed deer, wild turkeys, elk, raccoons, foxes, coyotes, and many other species. These creatures flourish in the protected atmosphere and wide wilderness of the national park.

It is advised to visit the park in the early morning or late evening when animals are most active to enhance your chances of seeing wildlife. There is a lot of wildlife in the Cades Cove region of the park, which is a well-liked tourist destination. Here, you might have the good fortune to see black bears searching for food, deer grazing in the fields, or even a glimpse of a coyote or red fox.

With more than 240 different species of birds, the Great Smoky Mountains National Park is a sanctuary for birdwatchers. Bird aficionados will have a great day seeing these feathery species, which include vivid warblers, majestic raptors, elusive owls, and vibrant woodpeckers. Numerous bird species are drawn to the park's different habitats, which include wetlands, meadows, and woodlands, throughout the year.

On the park's eastern side, in the Cataloochee Valley, you can go if you have a particular interest in elk. Visitors have the chance to get up close and personal with these majestic animals in this region, especially during the fall rutting season when the elk put on impressive dominance and wooing displays.

Remember that these creatures are wild and should be seen from a respectful distance to safeguard the safety and welfare of both tourists and wildlife. Avoid feeding or approaching the animals, keep a safe distance, and use binoculars or a zoom lens for up-close views.

Gatlinburg further provides educational programs and led excursions with a focus on animal observation and the local natural heritage. You will learn more about and develop a greater appreciation for the local wildlife when park rangers and local experts share information about the habitats and behavior of the animals.

Gatlinburg's abundant wildlife and the Great Smoky Mountains National Park offer an incredible opportunity to view and connect with the numerous animal species that call this area home, whether you are an experienced wildlife enthusiast or simply have a curiosity for the natural world.

## 3. Fishing:

In Gatlinburg, Tennessee, fishermen can unwind while reeling in their catches amid the scenic grandeur of the Great Smoky Mountains by engaging in the popular outdoor sport of fishing. Gatlinburg offers fantastic fishing options thanks to the abundance of rivers, streams, and lakes that are home to many different kinds of fish.

The Great Smoky Mountains National Park is one of the most well-liked fishing locations in the region. With more than 2,900 kilometers of pure streams, the park is a sanctuary for fly-fishing for trout. The streams of the area are home to native rainbow, brook, and brown trout, which anglers can try their luck catching.

Streams in the park fall into one of two categories: designated waterways or undesignated waters. Trout are routinely stocked in designated waters, providing constant fishing opportunities all year long. Undesignated waters, on the other hand, offer a more demanding and gratifying experience because they have trout populations that can support themselves there. A current Tennessee or North Carolina fishing license, which is simple to obtain, is necessary to go fishing in the national park.

Anglers of all ability levels can fish in some streams in the Gatlinburg region since they are conveniently located. The Little Pigeon River, which flows through the heart of Gatlinburg, is a well-liked fishing location for both novice and expert anglers. This river offers handy fishing opportunities close to the city's attractions and is routinely stocked.

Gatlinburg has a ton of undiscovered jewels for anglers looking for a more sedate and tranquil fishing experience. The Roaring Fork Motor Nature Trail and the Greenbrier region, for example, offer breathtaking scenery and a wealth of fishing options. Anglers can immerse themselves in nature while fishing in these tranquil areas' crystal-clear alpine streams.

Gatlinburg provides chances for lake and reservoir fishing in addition to stream fishing. Bass, crappie, and catfish populations are well-known in the nearby Douglas Lake and Cherokee Lake. These lakes have boat ramps and fishing piers, so boaters and shore fishermen can access them. A fantastic approach to exploring these lakes and improving your chances of a catch is to rent a boat or hire a fishing guide.

Gatlinburg provides fishing courses and guiding services if you're new to fishing or want to improve your abilities. The best fishing sites may be found with the help of knowledgeable guides, who can also provide you with expert advice and teach you various ways to enhance your fishing skills.

The Great Smoky Mountains National Park and its environs are subject to fishing laws, which include catch limitations and size restrictions. It's important to become aware of these rules and to fish ethically by respecting the environment and releasing unwanted or undersized fish.

Anglers of all ages and ability levels are guaranteed a pleasant fishing trip in Gatlinburg, whether they favor the solitude of mountain streams or the size of lakes. Gatlinburg is a place that appeals to both ardent anglers and those wishing to unwind in nature thanks to its abundance of fish species, breathtaking landscape, and reachable fishing areas.

## 4. Rafting in Whitewater

For thrill-seekers and nature lovers alike, whitewater rafting in Gatlinburg, Tennessee, offers an amazing journey. Gatlinburg is home to the Pigeon River, which is close to the Great Smoky Mountains and offers thrilling rapids and breathtaking scenery, making it a top spot for whitewater rafting.

Rafting on the Pigeon River can be done in a variety of parts, each of which is catered to a distinct ability level and inclination. For thrill-seekers looking for exhilarating whitewater action, the Upper Pigeon River, also known as the Upper Pigeon Gorge, is perfect. Class

III and IV rapids may be found in this area, giving you a heart-pounding thrill as you make your way through turbulent water and overcome exhilarating drops and waves.

The Lower Pigeon River is a great choice for those seeking a more relaxed rafting experience. This segment features quieter portions in between Class I and II rapids, making it suited for beginners and families. Participants can still take part in an enjoyable rafting excursion on the Lower Pigeon River while taking in the splendor of the nearby mountains and forests.

Rafting excursions on the Pigeon River are frequently guided, assuring everyone's safety and enjoyment. Your knowledgeable guides will provide you with instructions, safety briefings, and essential equipment, such as helmets and personal flotation devices (PFDs). They also serve as the rafts' captains and share their extensive knowledge of the river, its past, and the area.

Several outfitters in the Gatlinburg region provide whitewater rafting experiences on the Pigeon River. These outfitters provide a variety of trip options, such as half-day and full-day excursions, so you can pick the length and level of difficulty that best meets your interests. To make the most of your outdoor vacation, some outfitters even provide combo packages that incorporate other activities like zip-lining or horseback riding.

The Pigeon River's rafting season normally lasts from spring through fall, when the river levels are ideal. Depending on the weather and water flow from upstream dams, the precise timing may change. For the most recent information, contact the outfitters or check out their websites, and book reservations well in advance, especially during the busiest travel times.

In addition to giving you an adrenaline rush, whitewater rafting on the Pigeon River also enables you to get close to nature and experience the beauty of the surroundings. You'll experience spectacular vistas of the Great Smoky

Mountains as you navigate the rapids, spot wildlife along the riverbanks, and make enduring memories with your fellow rafters.

Whitewater rafting in Gatlinburg offers a memorable experience packed with adrenaline, stunning natural scenery, and the rush of overcoming the rapids, whether you're an experienced rafter or a first-time explorer. Prepare yourself to navigate, paddle, and fully immerse yourself in the exhilarating world of Gatlinburg whitewater rafting.

## 5. Ziplining:

In Gatlinburg, Tennessee, ziplining offers an exhilarating and distinctive way to take in the Great Smoky Mountains' breathtaking scenery. Gatlinburg provides the ideal setting for an exciting ziplining journey with its breathtaking scenery and thick forests.

Ziplining entails enjoying a thrilling adrenaline rush and admiring beautiful aerial views as you glide through the air on a hanging rope that is fastened to a harness. There is something for everyone in Gatlinburg thanks to the numerous ziplining courses available, which are catered to different preferences and skill levels.

The platforms and lines that make up these ziplining courses are often connected across the forest canopy. A safe and pleasurable experience is ensured by trained guides who give safety instructions, guarantee proper equipment usage, and accompany participants throughout the course.

You will get the chance to speed through the trees, glide over valleys, and take in expansive views of the surrounding mountains as you set off on a ziplining excursion in Gatlinburg. A thrilling experience that completely immerses you in the beauty and majesty of the natural surroundings is the feeling of freedom and the rush of wind as you zip from one level to another.

Many ziplining tours in Gatlinburg also include educational components, providing details on the region's history, geology, native flora and animals, and more. This gives participants a well-rounded experience that blends learning with adventure and enables them to develop a greater appreciation for nature.

Some ziplining courses can have extra components like elevated platforms, rappelling stations, or sky bridges that add to the difficulty and excitement. Your ziplining excursion will be a thrill you won't soon forget thanks to these added touches.

Gatlinburg's ziplining courses offer a safe and exhilarating adventure in a breathtaking natural setting, regardless of your level of expertise or whether you're a seasoned pro. Families, friendship groups, and solitary adventurers can all participate in this thrilling activity together because the courses are often made to accommodate people of different ages and physical abilities.

It's significant to remember that safety comes first on ziplining courses, and participants are given the required safety gear, such as helmets and harnesses. The guides are experienced specialists who make sure the right safety procedures are followed at all times.

Check the age and weight requirements, make reservations in advance, and dress in appropriate clothing and footwear for comfort and safety while organizing your ziplining excursion in Gatlinburg.

Gatlinburg's ziplining offers a distinctive vantage point on the Great Smoky Mountains' breathtaking scenery. You may make priceless memories while feeling the rush of flying through the treetops since it blends the excitement of adventure with the breathtaking beauty of nature. Prepare to soar, experience the rush of adrenaline, and enjoy the freedom of ziplining in Gatlinburg's gorgeous surroundings.

## 6. Mounted Riding:

In Gatlinburg, Tennessee, horseback riding is a fantastic opportunity to experience the breathtaking majesty of the

Great Smoky Mountains while getting in touch with nature and having a relaxing trip. All ages and skill levels of riders can find a variety of horseback riding adventures in Gatlinburg.

You can immerse yourself in the peaceful ambiance of the Smoky Mountains and take in a distinctive perspective of the surrounding surroundings by riding the routes. The trails provide stunning views of the majestic mountains as they meander through dense forests and are next to bubbling streams.

Gatlinburg offers a variety of guided horseback riding opportunities to make sure that riders have a fun and safe time. Experienced leaders show the route, giving directions, imparting knowledge about the region's flora and fauna, and assuring the safety of both riders and horses at all times.

Gatlinburg's horseback riding options cater to riders of all skill levels, whether you're an experienced horseback rider or a novice. The guides and crew are skilled at working with riders of various ability levels, and they choose horses according to each rider's degree of comfort and skill.

There are guided walking trail rides available for novices or those seeking a leisurely journey. These rides take you down beautiful routes at a leisurely pace, letting you soak in the scenery and forge a bond with your horse.

Gatlinburg additionally provides guided trail rides that involve trotting or even cantering for riders looking for a little more excitement and a faster pace. These rides offer a more thrilling experience while still assuring safety and enjoyment and are best suited for intermediate to expert riders.

With possibilities for individual rides, group rides, and even sultry trips for couples, Gatlinburg's horseback riding excursions are frequently adaptable. A very spectacular and unforgettable experience in the mountains is provided by some stables' unique rides offered at sunrise or sunset.

It's crucial to be aware that horseback riding may have weight restrictions, and bookings are normally advised to guarantee your seat. It is advised to bring sunscreen, bug spray, a camera, long pants, and closed-toed shoes to enjoy the scenic views along the trails.

In Gatlinburg, horseback riding offers a special and fun way to see the Great Smoky Mountains' natural splendor, bond with kind and well-cared-for horses, and establish a connection with nature. Horseback riding in Gatlinburg offers an unforgettable experience that will make lasting memories, whether you're a horse lover, a nature enthusiast, or just looking for a serene and gorgeous excursion.

## 7. Golfing:

For golf fans, playing golf in Gatlinburg, Tennessee, offers a fun outdoor activity amidst the scenic Smoky Mountains. Gatlinburg and the surrounding area are home to many outstanding golf courses that welcome players of all skill levels and provide a wonderful round of golf.

Gatlinburg's golf courses are renowned for their breathtaking scenery, with verdant fairways set against the backdrop of the spectacular mountains. The natural splendor gives your golf game a new perspective and makes the teeing-off experience peaceful and beautiful.

The Gatlinburg Golf Course, located in the foothills of the Great Smoky Mountains, is one of the area's well-known golf courses. This 18-hole course offers tough greens, undulating fairways, and strategically positioned bunkers for a fun and rewarding golfing experience. The stunning mountain views all around the course contribute to the game's overall atmosphere.

The Bent Creek Golf Course is another well-known golf course in the area. This course, which is located close to Cosby, is well-known for both its difficult design and picturesque surroundings. Bent Creek provides a magnificent site for golfers to test their skills. It is surrounded by tall trees and mountain streams. The course offers a distinctive and entertaining golfing experience with its tree-lined fairways, rolling topography, and water hazards.

The Sevierville Golf Club and the River Islands Golf Club are two additional neighboring courses that golfers visiting Gatlinburg might check out. These golf courses provide a variety of possibilities for golf aficionados to participate in their favorite sport by offering various layouts, difficulties, and picturesque perspectives.

Golfers may anticipate first-rate facilities and amenities in Gatlinburg in addition to the magnificent surroundings. Driving ranges, practice areas, manicured greens, and fully stocked pro shops are common amenities on golf courses. For golfers wishing to hone their skills or newcomers looking to learn the game, several courses also provide golf instruction and clinics.

Gatlinburg's golf courses are open to amateurs as well as professionals. Golfers of all ability levels, including novices and families, are welcome in the region. The golf courses in Gatlinburg offer an inviting and welcoming ambiance, regardless of whether you're an experienced player looking for a demanding round or a beginner looking to enjoy a relaxing game.

To guarantee availability, it is advised to book tee times in advance, particularly during busy times of the year. Additionally, when playing a round of golf, golfers should observe course etiquette, abide by local laws, and respect the environment.

Gatlinburg's golf courses offer a special fusion of exercise, leisure, and scenic beauty. Golfers can enjoy a very unforgettable round of golf at the Smoky Mountains, which offers picturesque courses, difficult layouts, and a tranquil setting.

## 8. Snowboarding and Skiing:

near the heart of the Great Smoky Mountains, near Gatlinburg, Tennessee, skiers, and snowboarders may enjoy exhilarating winter activities. The adjacent Ober Gatlinburg Ski Resort and Amusement Park provides a wonderful winter sports experience even though Gatlinburg town lacks ski resorts.

You can drive or take a magnificent aerial tramway to get to Ober Gatlinburg, which is only a short distance from the center of Gatlinburg. The resort offers both novice and expert skiers and snowboarders a variety of ski slopes and trails. Ober Gatlinburg has something to offer everyone, whether you're an experienced shredder or a beginner.

Modern snowmaking technology is installed on the Ober Gatlinburg ski slopes to provide the best skiing conditions even when there is little to no natural precipitation. The resort provides a variety of terrain, including easy slopes for novices, demanding runs for experienced riders looking for an exhilarating ride, and intermediate tracks for those trying to enhance their skills.

For snowboarders looking to show off their tricks and talents, Ober Gatlinburg offers a terrain park in addition to the ski slopes. Jumps, rails, boxes, and other features in the terrain park are intended to test and amuse snowboarders of all skill levels. To give riders a fun and secure environment in which to perfect their abilities and enjoy freestyle snowboarding, the park is routinely upgraded and maintained.

Equipment rental options are available at Ober Gatlinburg, making it simple for guests to acquire ski and snowboard equipment locally. The rental shop offers a large assortment of high-quality gear to meet your demands, whether you need skis, snowboards, boots, or helmets. The resort also provides ski and snowboard lessons for novices as well as those wishing to improve their technique under the guidance of qualified instructors.

Ober Gatlinburg provides many family-friendly winter activities in addition to skiing and snowboarding. On the indoor ice rink, you may enjoy ice skating; on the alpine slide, you can experience a thrilling ride; or on the snow tubing hill, you can have fun sliding down chutes coated with snow.

It's crucial to dress for the weather when visiting Ober Gatlinburg, with warm layers, water-resistant clothing, and appropriate footwear. To defend against the cold and the sun, sunscreen, goggles, and gloves are also necessary.

The Great Smoky Mountains, where Gatlinburg is situated, make for a stunning backdrop for skiing and snowboarding. It's a well-liked wintertime vacation spot for outdoor enthusiasts because of the slopes covered with snow, the breathtaking scenery, and the variety of thrilling winter activities.

Gatlinburg's proximity to Ober Gatlinburg Ski Resort guarantees an exciting winter adventure full of fun, excitement, and memories that will last a lifetime, whether you're an experienced skier or snowboarder or someone eager to try these thrilling sports for the first time.

# Chapter 8: Dining and shopping

## 1. Shopping in Gatlinburg's Downtown:

Visitors from all walks of life can enjoy a lovely and exciting shopping experience in downtown Gatlinburg. This little mountain town, which is nestled in the Great Smoky Mountains, has a large selection of distinctive boutiques, specialty stores, and galleries that appeal to a range of tastes and interests. Downtown Gatlinburg has everything you're looking for, whether you're looking for the ideal memento, locally crafted crafts, or to update your wardrobe with chic mountain fashion.

A plethora of businesses selling a wide variety of goods may be found as you meander around the busy streets. There is plenty to capture every shopper's interest, from charming gift shops packed with amusing items to art galleries showing the works of renowned local artists. Discover the beautiful boutiques that line the streets, each one inviting you to walk inside and indulge in a world of retail therapy with its vibrant displays and friendly doors.

If you enjoy outdoor exploration, you can find shops that are designed with outdoor enthusiasts in mind. To make sure you're well-equipped for your tour of the nearby natural treasures, these shops are supplied with the best hiking gear, camping gear, and tough clothing. The outdoor gear stores in Downtown Gatlinburg provide everything you need, whether you're planning an exciting whitewater rafting excursion or setting out on a hiking trek in the Great Smoky Mountains National Park.

If you have a sweet taste, Gatlinburg has a ton of candy shops and confectioneries that are guaranteed to sate your needs. Enjoy exquisite fudge, delicious handcrafted chocolates, and a variety of other enticing goodies. Try some locally produced jams, jellies, and preserves that are ideal for carrying a little bit of Gatlinburg with you.

The numerous art galleries dotted throughout Downtown Gatlinburg will fascinate art lovers. These exhibition spaces feature a wide variety of artistic genres and media, from classical paintings and sculptures to modern mixed-media works. Take your time to appreciate the skill on show, and consider bringing home a one-of-a-kind work of art to remember your trip.

As you browse the shops, you'll also come across quaint antique shops that are filled to the brim with antiques and collectibles. Discover hidden treasures, peruse nostalgic memorabilia, and travel back in time as you browse these fascinating emporiums. The antique shops in Downtown Gatlinburg will catch your interest whether you're an enthusiastic collector or just appreciate the excitement of finding something genuinely unique.

You'll get hungry after a satisfying day of shopping. Fortunately, Downtown Gatlinburg offers a diversified culinary scene that pleases all palates, making it a haven for foodies as well. There is a restaurant or bistro to suit every taste, with anything from foreign cuisine to Southern comfort food.

Spend a satisfying supper at one of the town's well-known barbecue restaurants, where you can indulge in mouthwatering ribs, pulled pork, and all the fixings. If you're craving seafood, savor the local Smoky Mountain area's fresh catches, expertly prepared and delivered with a side of Southern charm.

Gatlinburg is home to several eateries that dish up authentic Appalachian cuisine for visitors looking for a taste of the mountains. Try some of the delicious smoked meats, cornbread, and country-fried steak that honor the area's rich culinary tradition.

There are many cafés, diners, and sandwich shops in Downtown Gatlinburg if you're searching for a quick snack or a casual dining experience. Grab a gourmet burger, indulge in a slice of pizza, or relish a delectable sandwich crafted with ingredients that are obtained locally. There are countless possibilities, so you can find something to sate any craving.

## 2. The local Stores:

Any shopper visiting Gatlinburg should be sure to stop by The Village Shops. The Village, a quaint and attractive environment like a European village, is a short distance from the busy streets of downtown. The charming architecture, brick walkways, and lovely landscaping of this commercial area make for a distinctive and enjoyable shopping experience.

A calm and welcoming atmosphere will meet you as soon as you step inside The Village. A variety of charming houses and stores are connected by cobblestone walkways containing a range of boutiques, restaurants, and specialty stores. It's the ideal setting for a relaxing afternoon of touring because the atmosphere is both warm and alluring.

The abundance of boutique shops, each offering a unique range of goods, is one of The Village Shops' features. You'll find lots of possibilities to update your wardrobe or discover the ideal present for a loved one, from chic apparel businesses presenting the newest current trends to stores specializing in unique accessories and jewelry.

The Village has galleries displaying the works of regional and local artists, which art lovers will admire. Admire the magnificent sculptures, paintings, and other works of art at your leisure while soaking up the tranquil ambiance all around you. These galleries offer a chance to admire the skill and originality of the regional art scene, whether you're an art collector or just appreciate good craftsmanship.

The Village also caters to people looking for unique finds and specialty goods. Discover stores that sell pottery, handmade crafts, and home furnishings so you can incorporate a little of Gatlinburg's distinctive appeal into your living area. Find locally produced candles, soaps, and other handcrafted goods that are ideal for gifts or as mementos of your visit to the Smoky Mountains.

Spend some time unwinding in one of The Village's quaint cafes or eateries after a long day of shopping. Enjoy a tasty pastry, or a cup of freshly brewed coffee, or indulge in a leisurely lunch while taking in the tranquil atmosphere. The outdoor seating areas offer a peaceful haven where you may relax and think back on your shopping discoveries.

The Village holds numerous events and festivals all year long, enhancing the already bright and bustling ambiance. There is always something going on that improves the shopping experience, from live music performances to holiday celebrations. Keep an eye out for unique deals, events, and activities that will make your trip to The Village even more enjoyable.

The Village Shops in Gatlinburg offer a lovely break from the rush and bustle of daily life, whether you're an experienced shopper or simply appreciate visiting unusual and charming places. Enjoy the enchanting shopping experience it has to offer as you lose yourself in its comfortable atmosphere, find hidden treasures, and make memorable memories.

## 3. Loop for Arts & Crafts:

For art lovers, history aficionados, and anybody looking for an authentic and immersive artistic experience, Gatlinburg's Arts and Crafts Loop is a refuge. Just outside of downtown Gatlinburg, along this eight-mile picturesque drive, lives a community of craftspeople who have been producing and displaying their wares for decades. As you go through the Arts and Crafts Loop, you'll experience a sense of time travel and get to see the enduring craftsmanship of the Appalachian Mountains.

Over 100 studios, galleries, and shops can be found throughout the circle, each of which provides a different window into the world of handmade goods. You'll come across woodworkers, potters, weavers, glassblowers, and other skilled artists working on their skills in front of your eyes as you travel the meandering path. You can see the precise methods and devotion used to craft each handmade piece through this interactive experience.

Along the loop, woodworking is a common craft, with artists specializing in carving, cabinetry, and furniture construction. Visit their workshops to see the expertly created furniture, colorful bowls, and hand-carved sculptures that highlight the beauty of natural wood. You could even get to see how skilled craftspeople turn plain pieces of wood into magnificent works of art.

Pottery lovers will enjoy the wealth of studios along the loop's length. Enter these studios to see the fascinating process of molding clay into beautiful objects and elaborate pottery. You can choose from a broad variety of pottery styles and techniques, each with its special charm, ranging from useful mugs and plates to gorgeous vases and sculptures.

The Arts and Crafts Loop also has a significant presence for textile and fiber arts. Visit weaving workshops to see experienced weavers at work on looms producing colorful textiles, rugs, and tapestries. Observe the complex designs and striking hues that showcase the rich history of Appalachian weaving techniques.

Another fascinating craft you'll come across on the loop is glassblowing. Observe the amazing dance of molten glass as it turns into delicate vases, vibrant ornaments, and other stunning glass creations by entering a glassblower's workshop. A process explanation and any questions you may have will usually be provided by knowledgeable craftspeople, making it an interesting and educational experience.

The Arts and Crafts Loop is home to attractive galleries and stores where you may browse and buy one-of-a-kind handmade items in addition to the studios and workshops. These businesses display the wide variety of artistic expressions present in the neighborhood, from jewelry and pottery to paintings and sculptures. Explore the collections at your own pace, talk to the artists, and discover the ideal piece for you.

You'll have the chance to take in the area's natural beauty as you travel the Arts and Crafts Loop. The loop's natural surroundings give stunning vistas of the Smoky Mountains and a serene setting for your creative endeavors.

The Arts and Goods Loop in Gatlinburg offers a wholly immersive experience, regardless of whether you're a collector, an art aficionado, or simply admire the beauty of handmade goods. Experience the world of traditional Appalachian craftsmanship firsthand, see the wonder of artisans at work, and take something from the rich artistic legacy of the area home to be treasured for years to come.

## 4. Farmers' Market in Gatlinburg:

Locals and tourists alike congregate at the Gatlinburg Farmers Market in search of the freshest vegetables, handcrafted goods, and a genuine taste of the area's agricultural riches. This outdoor market, which is situated in the center of Gatlinburg, offers a wonderful chance to get to know local producers, craftspeople, and vendors while taking in the lively local vibe.

The Gatlinburg Farmers Market, which is open seasonally, offers an outstanding selection of farm-fresh fruits, vegetables, herbs, and flowers. You will be welcomed by an abundance of vibrant produce, alluring scents, and welcoming vendors ready to share their expertise and passion for their goods as you browse the market stalls. The market provides a wide variety of seasonal delights, allowing you to enjoy the flavors of the area at their peak freshness. These delights range from plump heirloom tomatoes and crisp lettuce to luscious peaches and sweet corn.

The farmers market is a veritable gold mine of handcrafted goods and locally created goods in addition to fresh food. Visit the stalls where homemade jams, jellies, and preserves prepared from regional fruits are sold. Learn about distinctive honey brews from the Smoky Mountains, each with a special flavor character.

Try freshly baked bread, pastries, and other mouthwatering goodies produced by skilled local artists.

The market is a focal point for handcrafted goods that highlight the imagination and expertise of regional artists. Beautifully created pottery, handcrafted soaps and candles, complex woodwork, and other one-of-a-kind crafts that are ideal for gifts or mementos are all to be found here. Get to know the craftspeople, discover their methods, and discover the area's rich cultural past.

The Gatlinburg Farmers Market offers more than just an abundance of fresh vegetables and handcrafted goods; it also fosters a lively, neighborhood-focused ambiance. At the market, entertainment and educational possibilities are frequently offered through live music performances, cooking demos, and educational programs. Talk to the farmers and sellers to learn more about sustainable agricultural methods, eating in season, and the significance of promoting local agriculture.

By going to the Gatlinburg Farmers Market, you can not only savor the local cuisine but also support regional farmers and businesses, promote sustainable agriculture, and strengthen community ties. It is a bustling community hub that honors the bounty of the land and the commitment of those who cultivate it.

The Gatlinburg Farmers Market is a must-visit location whether you're looking for fresh ingredients for a home-cooked dinner, want to learn about the local culture, or just want to take in the lively atmosphere of a bustling market. Explore this thriving exhibition of regional agriculture and craftsmanship while embracing the tastes, customs, and sense of community.

## 5. Restaurants and Regional Food:

Gatlinburg has a diverse restaurant industry that honors the tastes of the South and the Smoky Mountains when it comes to regional food. There is something for every pallet, from substantial comfort cuisine to scrumptious BBQ and delectable sweet desserts. Let's examine some of Gatlinburg's top restaurants and local culinary delights.

**i. Comfort food from the South**

Gatlinburg is renowned for its delectable Southern comfort cuisine. Enjoy traditional foods like creamy macaroni and cheese, country-fried beef, and fried chicken. These hearty foods are served in some Gatlinburg restaurants that specialize in doing so, frequently with a dash of charm and Southern hospitality.

**ii. Barbecue:**

If you go to Gatlinburg, you must try the barbeque there. Take a bite out of savory brisket, pulled pork, and soft, smokey ribs. Look for barbecue restaurants that have skilled pitmasters and special spice rubs to guarantee a mouthwatering experience. In addition to classic sides like cornbread, coleslaw, and baked beans, many of these restaurants now provide a barbecue.

**iii. Succulent mountain trout:**

Gatlinburg is a great place to eat fresh mountain trout because it is surrounded by gorgeous rivers and streams.

This delicacy is frequently served in local restaurants in a variety of preparations, such as simply grilled or pan-fried with butter and herbs. Experience the genuine flavor of the Smoky Mountains by indulging in the exquisite nuances of this local delicacy.

**iv. Authentic Appalachian food:**

Through its food, Gatlinburg celebrates its Appalachian roots. Watch out for eateries that serve food based on age-old Appalachian recipes. Ramps (wild leeks), sorghum molasses, cornmeal, and other foraged foods might be used in these meals. Explore these distinctive Appalachian flavors as you embrace the area's rich history and culinary traditions.

**v. Sweet Snacks**

Gatlinburg is a haven for anyone who loves sweet things. Try the handcrafted fudge, smooth ice cream, and delicious candies at one of the many candy shops and confectioneries dotted about the town. To satisfy your sweet need, indulge in traditional flavors or experiment with unusual pairings like salted caramel or maple pecan.

**vi. Breweries of local craft beer**

Gatlinburg is also home to many regional craft breweries that provide aficionados with a wide selection of artisanal beers to sample. These breweries highlight the diversity and excellence of the regional brewing sector with their hoppy IPAs, deep stouts, and refreshing wheat beers. Experience the tastes created by enthusiastic brewers by taking a tour of the brewery and tasting a flight of beers.

Gatlinburg has a wide range of dining venues that may accommodate a variety of tastes and preferences. There is something for everyone, from fine dining to family-friendly restaurants and informal cafes. Discover quaint eateries that offer mouthwatering fare and welcoming Southern hospitality as you wander the streets of downtown Gatlinburg and beyond.

Keep in mind to search for neighborhood favorites and suggestions since the food scene is subject to change. Gatlinburg provides a gastronomic experience that will leave you satiated and hankering for more, whether you're looking for traditional Southern cuisine, local delicacies, or flavors from around the world.

## 6. Distilleries and Breweries:

Gatlinburg is renowned for its booming craft beer and spirits sector in addition to its breathtaking natural beauty and recreational activities. Numerous breweries and distilleries in the area provide tourists the option to sample locally produced drinks and take in the craftsmanship involved in their creation. Let's explore the breweries and distilleries in Gatlinburg:

**1. The Gatlinburg Brewing Co.**

For fans of beer, Gatlinburg Brewing Company is a well-known location. This microbrewery uses a combination of conventional brewing methods and cutting-edge flavors to produce a wide variety of craft beers. Their constantly changing assortment guarantees that there is always something new to drink, ranging from velvety stouts and crisp beers to hoppy IPAs. Visit their taproom to have a drink, visit the brewery, and see how they create their beer.

**2. Brewery Smoky Mountain**

A local favorite, Smoky Mountain Brewery is renowned for its handcrafted beers and relaxed atmosphere. Lagers, ales, and specialty beers are among the year-round and seasonal beverages that they provide. Delicious pub fares like wood-fired pizza, burgers, and wings go well with your beer. It's simple to locate a Smoky Mountain Brewery to quench your thirst and sate your appetite thanks to its numerous sites in Gatlinburg and surrounding Pigeon Forge.

**3. Moonshine by Ole Smoky**

Ole Smoky Moonshine offers a genuine flavor of this tradition, which is firmly ingrained in the history and culture of the Appalachian region. This distillery, which is located in the heart of Gatlinburg, provides a wide range of moonshine varieties, from traditional selections like original corn whiskey to unusual infusions like apple pie and blackberry. Learn how to make moonshine during a tour of the distillery, try several flavors, and even catch live music performances in the courtyard outside.

**4. Company called Sugarlands Distilling:**

Another well-known distillery in Gatlinburg is Sugarlands Distilling Company, which produces moonshine and specialty spirits. They have a wide variety of flavors available, including popular ones like peach and butter pecan. A variety of premium whiskeys and rums are also produced by Sugarlands Distilling Company, displaying the craftsmanship and care put into each bottle. Visit a distillery, partake in sampling, and learn about the tastes that best represent the Smoky Mountains.

**5. Nashville Cider Company**

Tennessee Cider Company offers a cool alternative for individuals who prefer cider. This cidery, which is in

Gatlinburg, specializes in small-batch, handcrafted ciders created from regional apples. Their selection includes everything from classic dry ciders to cutting-edge fruit-infused blends, satisfying a range of palates. Visit their tasting room to try their ciders and see how they are made.

It's important to plan for transportation while visiting Gatlinburg's breweries and distilleries. You can sample a range of flavors at several establishments and choose your favorites by taking advantage of the tasting flights or samples they offer.

# Chapter 9: Festivals and Events

## 1. Fourth of July midnight procession in Gatlinburg:

Both locals and visitors are enthralled by the remarkable Gatlinburg Fourth of July Midnight Parade. The picturesque city of Gatlinburg, which is tucked away amid the Great Smoky Mountains, comes to life with a colorful and memorable parade as the clock strikes midnight and the country gets ready to celebrate its independence.

The Fourth of July is a highly celebrated festival in the US, denoting liberty and nationalism. With its twist—the midnight parade—Gatlinburg, which is renowned for its spectacular natural beauty and gracious hospitality, elevates this celebration to new heights. While most cities choose to hold their parades in the morning or the evening, Gatlinburg chose to host its parade at the stroke of midnight, which adds a special touch of excitement and magic that makes it stand out from the rest.

The brilliance of the pyrotechnics above and the jubilant spirit of the spectators below illuminate the streets of Gatlinburg as the parade route winds through them. The atmosphere is electric with anticipation as the first marching bands and floats make their way through the crowd.

The patriotic spectacle is one of the hallmarks of the Gatlinburg Fourth of July midnight parade. The parade honors the nation's rich history and the sacrifices made by its citizens by featuring depictions of historical figures and events alongside traditional American symbols like the flag and the bald eagle.

Each of the intricately painted and crafted floats tells a different tale. Local companies, associations, and community organizations use their creativity to create eye-catching displays that respect American traditions and ideals. The floats captivate the audience with their vivid colors, lively characters, and extravagant props, leaving them in awe and admiration.

Marching bands from near and far accompany the floats, filling the nighttime air with heartfelt lyrics and infectious rhythm. The musicians' skill and accuracy produce a symphony of sound that touches the audience's hearts. People start to sway to the music as the joyous atmosphere pervades the streets, lifting their spirits.

The sky explodes with a breathtaking fireworks show as the parade moves forward. The colorful explosions and crackling sounds high above give the celebrations an additional air of grandeur. The parade is set against an amazing backdrop of fireworks, which give a mystical glow over the floats and entertainers and capture everyone in attendance's attention and imagination.

The Gatlinburg Fourth of July Midnight Parade is a celebration of community, camaraderie, and the American spirit in addition to the country's freedom. It serves as a reminder of the principles that unite us as a country and the joy we all feel in being a member of this wonderful nation.

The procession is a once-in-a-lifetime event for locals and guests. As they take in the joyful mood, families get together, friends get together, and strangers make friends. Young and old alike can be seen lining the streets in anticipation of the procession of floats, bands, and performers. The night is filled with a symphony of celebration as laughter, shouting, and applause.

The Gatlinburg Fourth of July midnight celebration includes a wide range of activities and festivities in addition to the parade. Visitors can stroll through the city's quaint center, peruse art galleries, savor delectable regional food, and take in the natural splendor of the Great Smoky Mountains.

## 2. Winter Wonder in Gatlinburg:

The picturesque city of Gatlinburg is transformed into a winter paradise during the festival known as Gatlinburg

Winter Magic. Gatlinburg comes alive with brilliant lights, Christmas decorations, and a variety of fun events that capture the wonder and spirit of the holiday season from the minute the first snowflakes fall upon the Great Smoky Mountains.

The breathtaking display of millions of glittering LED lights that cover the streets, buildings, and trees all around the city serves as the focal point of Gatlinburg Winter Magic. The display, which transforms Gatlinburg into a brilliant wonderland of colors and patterns, is nothing short of stunning. The lights, which range from vivid archways and flowing light curtains to whimsical characters and nature-inspired designs, produce a fascinating ambiance that inspires wonder and joy in visitors.

It will seem as though you have entered a scene from a book as you stroll through the lit-up streets. The clean snow reflects the lights, creating a cozy and inviting glow that beckons you to continue exploring. The displays and decorations are painstakingly made, displaying the community's creativity and commitment to the event.

The Trolley Ride of Lights is one of Gatlinburg Winter Magic's highlights. A festively painted trolley is available for visitors to ride, and they can travel magically through the shining streets. For families, groups of friends, and couples, the trolley trip gives a special vantage position from which to take in the exquisite light displays as well as a comfortable and enjoyable experience.

Beyond the lights, Gatlinburg Winter Magic provides a wide range of entertainment options. Throughout the festival, the city holds unique concerts, seasonal festivals, and performances. Live music performances, Christmas parades, and even a visit from Santa Claus are all available to visitors. Every aspect of Gatlinburg is infused with the holiday spirit, which fosters a convivial and upbeat environment that unites people.

Gatlinburg's distinctive boutiques, artisan stores, and specialized shops will please shoppers. The downtown area is transformed into a winter market, selling a variety of handcrafted goods, seasonal accents, and unique presents. There is something for everyone on your holiday shopping list, from handcrafted decorations to homemade fudge and everything in between.

Gatlinburg Winter Magic offers many possibilities to discover the local natural beauty for those seeking outdoor pursuits. The Great Smoky Mountains National Park offers stunning scenic drives, beautiful hiking paths, and the opportunity to experience the allure of snow-covered vistas. To make the most of the winter season, outdoor enthusiasts can participate in activities like skiing, snowboarding, and tubing.

Gatlinburg Winter Magic is a time when foodies will also be in culinary nirvana. The city is home to a wide variety of establishments that serve up delectable holiday-themed delicacies, classic Southern comfort food, and fine dining. Gatlinburg's culinary scene has something to please every palate, whether you're in the mood for warm apple cider, savory mountain fish, or decadent desserts.

Gatlinburg Winter Magic is more than simply a festival; it's a celebration of the holiday season, the neighborhood, and the delight of getting to know one another. Families get together to make cherished memories, friends get together to laugh and be merry, and people from near and far travel to take part in the magic of the season. The event embodies the true spirit of the holidays with its warmth, love, and feeling of amazement.

## 3. Songs and legends from the Smoky Mountains:

Smoky Mountains Tunes and Tales is an engaging event that uses music, storytelling, and interactive performances to vividly depict the Great Smoky Mountains' rich history. This distinctive festival gives guests a peek into the regional cultural customs and folklore and is held in the picturesque city of Gatlinburg, which is tucked away in the majesty of the Smokies.

Local musicians, storytellers, and artists with a strong connection to the Smoky Mountains' tradition and history are included at the festival. You'll come across a variety of historical-era people as you stroll around Gatlinburg's streets, each having an engrossing tale to share. These artists, who range from itinerant minstrels and Appalachian balladeers to accomplished artisans and vivacious dancers, capture the essence and customs of the highlands.

The air is filled with the melodies of traditional Appalachian music, which carries visitors back in time. Banjo players, fiddlers, and guitarists trade songs that have been passed down through the years, bringing authenticity and a sense of nostalgia. With tales of love, grief, and the untamed beauty of the Smokies, the sincere lyrics and beautiful melodies convey the essence of life in the mountains.

At Smoky Mountains Tunes and Tales, storytelling takes center stage alongside the music. In the Appalachian region, the art of storytelling has long been revered as a tradition, and the festival honors this oral history by displaying gifted storytellers who enthrall audiences with their captivating tales. These storytellers take listeners to a realm of wonder and imagination, whether they are telling tales of historical occurrences, mythological creatures, or personal anecdotes.

The centerpiece of Smoky Mountains Tunes and Tales are interactive performances that let guests interact with the artists and fully experience the community. Cloggers and square dancers welcome attendees to join in the energetic foot-stomping fun, and traditional craftspeople showcase their weaving, blacksmithing, and pottery-making techniques. These practical encounters help people have a deeper understanding of the artistry and craftsmanship that have shaped the area's legacy.

You'll have the chance to speak with the performers and discover the Smoky Mountains' past and customs as you stroll through the festival. A friendly and welcoming environment that promotes a sense of community and connection is created by the artists' eagerness to share their expertise and personal experiences.

Smoky Mountains Tunes and Tales features a range of food vendors, artisan markets, and local businesses where you may find one-of-a-kind handmade goods, traditional Appalachian products, and mouthwatering regional cuisine. In addition to live performances and interactive activities. These products offer a sense of regional flavors and talents, from homemade jams and freshly baked foods to quilts and woodcarvings.

The festival not only showcases the diverse culture of the Smoky Mountains but also emphasizes how crucial it is to maintain and advance local customs. Smoky Mountains Tunes and Tales ensures the survival and inspiration of this priceless cultural heritage by exhibiting regional singers and artisans.

## 4. Fair of Craftspeople in Gatlinburg:

The Gatlinburg Craftsmen's Fair is a well-known occasion that highlights the extraordinary creativity and workmanship of craftspeople from all around the nation. This fair, which takes place in the exciting Tennessee city of Gatlinburg, has established itself as a top destination for people looking for one-of-a-kind, handcrafted items and a window into the world of accomplished artists.

The fair is held in the Gatlinburg Convention Center, which has been converted into a busy marketplace with booths and displays showcasing a variety of artistic mediums and styles. Every visitor will find something to pique their interest thanks to the fair's wide variety of crafts, which range from woodworking and pottery to textiles, jewelry, and metals.

The fair's heart and soul are the artisans who make its products. Based on their expertise, originality, and commitment to their craft, each exhibitor is chosen with care. You'll have the chance to interact with these gifted people as you stroll through the fair and discover their methods, sources of inspiration, and the narratives that led to their works.

You'll be treated to a visual feast of carefully made items as you browse the aisles. You'll be drawn to the beautiful wood carvings, the intricately decorated pottery, and the precisely woven textiles. It is a genuinely amazing experience because of the obvious passion and attention to detail put into each work.

The possibility to see live demonstrations by the artisans themselves is one of the Fair's distinctive features. As they shape, mold, and create exquisite pieces of art from raw materials, you can see for yourself how expertly they practice their skill. It is not only instructive but also utterly exciting to watch a potter turn clay on a wheel or a blacksmith forge metal with dexterity and ability.

Additionally, the fair provides a wonderful chance to personally support these skilled artisans by buying their works of art. There are many possibilities available, whether you're looking for a one-of-a-kind piece of jewelry, a handcrafted wooden bowl, or a gorgeous cloth. The event invites attendees to recognize the worth of handcrafted goods and to develop a close relationship with the creators of those goods.

The Gatlinburg Craftsmen's Fair includes extra diversions and entertainment in addition to the craft exhibitions. For guests of all ages, live musical performances, cultural exhibits, and hands-on activities offer a well-rounded experience. You can relish delectable delights as you explore the displays and exhibits at the fair because it frequently has food booths selling regional specialties.

The Gatlinburg Craftsmen's Fair not only honors talent and originality, but it also serves as a symbol of the value of maintaining traditional craftsmanship in the contemporary era. It gives craftsmen a stage on which to display their skills and guarantees that their crafts live on and are valued by the next generations.

## 5. Chilli Cook-off in Gatlinburg:

A thrilling culinary competition, the Gatlinburg Chili Cook-Off draws together chili connoisseurs from near and far to compete for the title of finest chili in town. This chili cook-off, which takes place in the center of Gatlinburg, Tennessee, highlights the inventiveness, flavors, and intense competitiveness of chili-making.

Participants set up their cooking stations and anxiously prepared their top-secret chili recipes throughout the event. Visitors are drawn in by the aroma of simmering spices and the promise of a tasty experience. You'll have the chance to sample a wide range of chili recipes as you progress through the cook-off, each of which offers a distinctive take on this traditional cuisine.

There is something for everyone's taste preferences at the Gatlinburg Chili Cook-Off thanks to the variety of categories, which include conventional chili, spicy chili, white chili, and even vegetarian chili. You're sure to find chili ideas that will sate your needs, whether you prefer a robust, meat-filled chili or a lighter, plant-based version.

Voting for your favorites while you sample the numerous chili submissions will give the event a more interactive and welcoming atmosphere. Attendees will also get the chance to interact with the participants, hear about their chili-making methods, and recognize the passion that goes into producing each pot of chili.

The Gatlinburg Chili Cook-Off features live music performances, entertainment, and activities for the whole family in addition to the chili tasting. Local sellers frequently erect booths where they provide tourists with a selection of treats, drinks, and crafts. This creates a lively and animated atmosphere where you may unwind, socialize, and take in the celebratory atmosphere of the event.

In addition to enjoying delectable chili, the cook-off also promotes charitable causes. The event is noteworthy and significant since a large portion of the revenues helps nonprofit groups, which benefits the neighborhood.

The Gatlinburg Chili Cook-Off honors culinary innovation, cordial competition, and teamwork. In a fun and inclusive setting, it brings together families, foodies, and chili aficionados. The Gatlinburg Chili Cook-Off promises a remarkable and enjoyable experience, whether you're a chili expert eager to sample distinctive and delectable recipes or simply someone who appreciates fantastic cuisine and a lively setting.

## 6. Wildflower Pilgrimage in Spring:

A nature lover's fantasy comes true during the Gatlinburg Spring Wildflowers Pilgrimage. This yearly celebration of the Great Smoky Mountains National Park's bright beauty and biodiversity is centered on the spectacular display of wildflowers that cover the area in the spring.

The pilgrimage draws tourists from all over, including nature lovers, botanists, photographers, and curious people who are eager to see the emergence of color and life as winter ends. An in-depth knowledge and appreciation of native wildflowers and the fragile ecosystems they inhabit are fostered in participants of the event through guided walks, educational seminars, workshops, and practical activities.

The guided treks that are led by knowledgeable professionals with a wealth of knowledge about the park's flora and wildlife are one of the highlights of the Spring Wildflowers Pilgrimage. These walks take hikers over beautiful pathways that take them to great areas when the wildflowers are in bloom. The guides provide intriguing information on the various wildflower species, their distinctive traits, and the ecological importance they hold within the park as visitors go along.

You will be treated to a kaleidoscope of hues as you travel the pathways as the wildflowers display their bright petals. The diversity of wildflowers on display is simply breathtaking, ranging from delicate trilliums and dazzling orchids to cheerful daisies and graceful violets. The guides will point out elusive and rare animals, enabling you to experience nature's wonders up close and take breathtaking pictures that you will treasure for years to come.

The Spring Wildflowers Pilgrimage includes a variety of educational seminars and workshops offered by specialists in botany, ecology, and conservation in addition to the guided hikes. In-depth discussions on the world of wildflowers are covered in these lectures, along with information on their life cycles, pollination techniques, and the value of protecting their natural habitats. Participants can learn more, ask questions, and get a greater understanding of the complex web of life that sustains these delicate blossoms.

Additionally, there are participatory activities for pilgrims of all ages. Families can participate in interactive workshops where kids can make crafts, play games, and view educational displays to learn about the value of wildflowers. These pursuits cultivate a love of the outdoors and teach environmental stewardship, inspiring future generations to save and conserve these natural wonders.

While the Great Smoky Mountains National Park's more extensive natural treasures are also celebrated at the Spring Wildflowers Pilgrimage, the event's primary focus is on the wildflowers. The treks and other activities may offer chances to see wildlife, take in beautiful views, and discover the geological aspects of the park, adding to the enjoyment and fostering a well-rounded exploration of the region's natural heritage.

The Spring Wildflowers Pilgrimage honors wildflowers' fleeting beauty and ecological importance. It serves as a reminder of how delicate these natural riches are and how crucial conservation efforts are to guarantee their existence for future generations. The occasion encourages awe, connection, and regard for the natural environment in addition to providing an immersive and informative experience.

# Chapter 10: Gatlinburg Day Trips

## 1. Pigeon Forge

Consider taking a trip to Pigeon Forge and the nearby attractions for a wonderful day trip from Gatlinburg. The natural beauty, family-friendly entertainment, and wide range of recreational opportunities in Pigeon Forge are well known. Here is a thorough schedule to make the most of your day trip:

**Morning:**

1. Visit the Great Smoky Mountains National Park Visitor Center in Pigeon Forge first thing in the morning. Learn as much as you can about the park, its trails, and any ongoing activities or displays.

2. Take a picturesque drive down the Newfound Gap Road, commonly known as U.S. Route 1, starting from the tourist center. Route 441. This route has various overlooks where you may stop and take great pictures

while providing stunning views of the Smoky Mountains.

3. Reach the Newfound Gap, which is located at an elevation of 1,538 meters (or 5,046 feet). To appreciate the park's natural beauty, go for a quick trek on one of the neighboring routes, such as the Appalachian Trail.

4. Following your hike, descend to Pigeon Forge and proceed to Old Mill Square. This historic district includes modest shops and eateries in addition to an operating gristmill from the 1800s.

**Afternoon:**

1. Visit Dollywood, a premier theme park owned by Dolly Parton, the queen of country music, for an adrenaline experience. Enjoy exhilarating rides, live music, and mouthwatering cuisine. A range of performances is available at Dollywood, including musical concerts, stunt acts, and ethnic demonstrations.

2. Visit the Titanic Museum Attraction if you want to learn more about the area's maritime history. This museum features interactive exhibits that let you experience the Titanic's history and tragedy in addition to housing a full-scale model of the ship.

3. Visit one of the many eateries in Pigeon Forge to grab some food. There are many alternatives available, ranging from regional specialties to global cuisines.

**Evening:**

1. Catch a dinner performance at one of Pigeon Forge's famed theaters after supper. Hatfield and McCoy Dinner Feud, Smoky Mountain Opry, and Pirates Voyage Dinner and Show are available options. These performances bring together fun, humor, music, and delectable cuisine for an unforgettable evening.

2. In Pigeon Forge, pay a visit to The Island to round out your day excursion. The Great Smoky Mountain Wheel, a tall Ferris wheel that gives expansive vistas of the region, is one of the attractions at this entertainment

complex, which also includes food and retail options. Enjoy taking a stroll through the exquisitely lighted streets while indulging in dessert or ice cream.

As you can see, Pigeon Forge provides an abundance of sights to see and things to do for an unforgettable day trip from Gatlinburg. This energetic town has something for everyone, whether your interests are in the outdoors, amusement parks, history, or entertainment. Have fun exploring Pigeon Forge and the area around it!

## 2. Disney World

You're in for a memorable experience if you're thinking about visiting Dollywood on a day trip from Gatlinburg. Dolly Parton, a prominent country music performer, is the owner of Dollywood, a renowned amusement park in Pigeon Forge. A suggested schedule for your day:

**Morning:**

1. To make the most of your time in the park, start your day early. For the best experience and to avoid the crowds, get to Dollywood as soon as it opens.

2. Starting with Showstreet, Rivertown Junction, Craftsman's Valley, and Wilderness Pass, explore the park's numerous themed zones. Take your time to savor the particular atmosphere and the finer points of each segment.

3. Take the renowned Dollywood Express from the Jukebox Junction area. You can enjoy beautiful views of the nearby Smoky Mountains as you travel through the park on this steam-engine train for 20 minutes.

4. Enjoy a great breakfast or lunch at one of the park's many restaurants after the train journey. Dollywood features a variety of restaurants to satiate your appetite, with everything from international cuisine to comfort food from the South.

**Afternoon:**

1. It's time to experience the exhilarating thrills and attractions that Dollywood has to offer after recharging. Everyone will find something to enjoy here, from water slides to roller coasters to family-friendly attractions.

2. Don't forget to ride the iconic coasters at Dollywood, including Lightning Rod, Wild Eagle, and Thunderhead. These heart-pounding rides include beautiful vistas, exciting twists, and turns.

3. Enjoy some of the park's unique experiences in between adrenaline rides. Explore the Chasing Rainbows Museum, which highlights Dolly Parton's life and work, or pay a visit to the Eagle Mountain Sanctuary, a natural habitat for non-releasable bald eagles.

4. At one of the park's many eateries, treat yourself to a hearty Southern-style lunch. The dining selections at Dollywood are likely to satiate your tastes, from barbecue to fried chicken and homestyle sides.

**Evening:**

1. Be sure to see some of the park's live performances and entertainment as the day goes on. The live shows of Dollywood are renowned for their excellence and frequently include actors, musicians, and dancers.

2. Take a spin on the Great Pumpkin Wheel, the Dollywood Ferris Wheel, to enjoy the evening. The park and its surroundings may be seen in exquisite detail from this towering attraction.

3. Before you leave, look around the Dollywood Emporium and other stores to locate one-of-a-kind trinkets, Dollywood memorabilia, and locally made crafts.

4. As your time at Dollywood draws to a close, you can decide whether to eat dinner at one of the park's eateries or return to Gatlinburg and eat at one of the many restaurants there.

Dollywood, which combines exhilarating rides, live entertainment, mouthwatering cuisine, and a dash of Southern charm, makes for an excellent day trip choice from Gatlinburg. Before your visit, make sure to check the park's schedule for any special events or performances. Have fun when visiting Dollywood.

## 3. Cades Cove

Explore Cades Cove if you're searching for a tranquil and beautiful day excursion from Gatlinburg. Cades Cove, a picturesque valley in the Great Smoky Mountains National Park, is well-known for its breathtaking scenery, abundant animals, and fascinating past. The following is a recommended schedule for your day trip to Cades Cove:

**Morning:**

1. To make the most of your time in Cades Cove, leave Gatlinburg as early in the day as possible. For breakfast, bring a picnic or pick up some treats at a nearby bakery.

2. The Townsend Gate to the Great Smoky Mountains National Park is the one that is most convenient for Cades Cove. As you travel to the valley, take in the scenic trip.

3. When you get to Cades Cove, go to the Cable Mill Historic Area first thing in the morning. Discover the

historic structures that have been restored, such as a running grist mill, a blacksmith shop, a smokehouse, and many barns. Discover the hardships and manner of life of the first settlers.

4. Visitor Center in Cades Cove offers bicycle rentals or strolls. On Saturdays and Wednesdays, the 11-mile (17.7-km) loop road around the valley is closed to cars until 10:00 AM, allowing you to take in the tranquility of the outdoors.

**Afternoon:**
1. The Cades Cove Loop Road, which offers breathtaking views of the mountains, meadows, and historic structures, can be cycled or driven further. Spend some time taking in the tranquility and beauty of the surroundings.

2. Keep an eye out for wildlife, as Cades Cove is renowned for having a wide variety of wildlife. There's a chance you'll see white-tailed deer, black bears, wild turkeys, coyotes, and different kinds of birds. When

viewing wildlife in a park, make sure to keep a safe distance and adhere to the rules.

3. Pick one or two Cades Cove hiking trails to investigate. The popular Abrams Falls Trail takes you on a leisurely 5-mile (8-kilometer) roundtrip hike to a beautiful waterfall. As an alternative, the 8.5-mile (13.7-km) Rich Mountain Loop Trail offers a loop through forests and meadows with stunning valley views.

4. At one of Cades Cove's designated picnic areas, enjoy a lunchtime picnic. Find a quiet area where you can enjoy your meal while admiring the breathtaking mountain views.

**Evening:**

1. Make your way back to Gatlinburg as your time in Cades Cove comes to an end. Think back on the tranquility and beauty of nature you encountered today.

2. To enjoy a filling dinner, think about visiting one of Gatlinburg's eateries. There are many choices, from Southern food to flavors from around the world.

3. After dinner, if you have the time and energy, stroll through Gatlinburg's busy streets. Take in some delectable ice cream or other sweet treats while exploring the stores, galleries, and attractions that line the Parkway.

A day trip to Cades Cove offers a peaceful retreat into nature and an opportunity to engage with the area's rich history. Bring water, sunscreen, comfy walking shoes, binoculars, and other items to enjoy the wildlife. Have fun exploring Cades Cove and the Great Smoky Mountains National Park's natural wonders!

## 4. Clingmans Dome

A day trip to Clingmans Dome should be at the top of your list if you're looking for breathtaking views and an overwhelming sense of beauty. With a height of 6,643 feet (2,025 meters), Clingmans Dome is the highest peak in the Great Smoky Mountains National Park. Here is a suggested itinerary for your day trip from Gatlinburg to Clingmans Dome:

**Morning:**

1. Early morning departure from Gatlinburg will give you plenty of time for exploration. For the trip, bring some snacks, water, and sunscreen.

2. As you travel towards Clingmans Dome along the Great Smoky Mountains National Park's scenic roads. Take in the beautiful scenery and keep an eye out for wildlife as you travel.

3. Approach the summit and arrive at the Clingmans Dome Visitor Center. Gather information about the surroundings, the state of the trail, and any advisories that are currently in effect.

4. Start your challenging but rewarding 0.8-kilometer (0.5-mile) hike to Clingmans Dome Observation Tower.

Take your time and enjoy the trip; the trail is paved but fairly steep. You'll pass by educational panels about the ecology and natural features of the park along the way.

**Midday:**

1. Get to the Clingmans Dome Observation Tower, a striking building with sweeping views of the valleys and mountains nearby. From the observation deck of the tower, take in the stunning views while admiring the beauty of nature and taking pictures.

2. Take quick strolls along the close-by trails as you explore the area around the tower. If you're up for a longer hike, the Forney Ridge Trail and the Appalachian Trail both pass through Clingmans Dome, offering opportunities for additional exploration.

3. At one of the designated picnic areas close to the Clingmans Dome Visitor Center, enjoy a picnic lunch. Enjoy your meal while taking in the tranquility of the surroundings.

**Afternoon:**

1. Consider the 4.4-mile (7.1-km) round-trip hike along the Forney Ridge Trail to Andrews Bald if you're up for more hiking. This walk is especially lovely in the spring and summer, leading to a magnificent grassy bald with breathtaking views.

2. Alternatively, if you'd rather spend the afternoon at your leisure, travel along the nearby Newfound Gap Road (U.S. Route 441) for a picturesque drive. There are numerous overlooks along this road where you can stop and take in the spectacular views of the Smoky Mountains.

**Evening:**

1. Return to Gatlinburg as the day draws to a close. Think back on the breathtaking views and experiences you made at Clingmans Dome.

2. Enjoy a wonderful dinner at one of Gatlinburg's eateries while sampling regional delicacies or other cuisines.

3. Take a stroll along the Parkway in Gatlinburg, examining the available stores, activities, and entertainment options, if you still have any energy.

A day trip to Clingmans Dome offers the chance to experience the grandeur of the Great Smoky Mountains up close and admire nature's beauty from one of the area's highest vantage points. Keep in mind to layer your clothing because it might get much colder at the summit than it does at lower heights. Enjoy your day discovering Clingmans Dome and the stunning national park surroundings!

## 5. The Arts and Crafts Loop in Gatlinburg

The Gatlinburg Arts and Crafts Loop is a must-visit location during your day trip from Gatlinburg if you have a passion for art and crafts. A thriving neighborhood of artists, craftspeople, and galleries may be found along this picturesque 8-mile (12.8-km) ring route. Here is a recommended route for visiting the Gatlinburg Arts and Crafts Loop:

**Morning:**

1. Start your day by traveling to the Gatlinburg Arts and Crafts Community, which is situated close to the city's center. The loop is easily reachable by car, short shuttle, cab journey, or by driving.

2. Start your artistic trip in the Great Smoky Arts & Crafts Community, which is home to the majority of American independent artists. The circle route is lined with numerous stores, studios, and galleries.

3. View the beautifully handcrafted pottery masterpieces from the Alewine Pottery studio. Browse the assortment of useful and beautiful ceramic pieces while watching the experienced craftspeople at work.

4. Visit the Little River Gem Mine, Paul Murray Gallery, and other studios and galleries that are situated throughout the circle to continue your adventure. Unique works of art, including paintings, sculptures, jewelry, woodwork, and more, are available at each stop.

**Midday:**

1. Visit one of the quaint eateries or cafés located within the Gatlinburg Arts & Crafts Community for lunch. Numerous restaurants provide delicious options for a quick snack or a leisurely supper.

2. As you savor your meal, observe the neighborhood's atmosphere and engage in discussion with the local artisans. They frequently enjoy sharing the methods, sources of inspiration, and narratives that went into their works.

**Afternoon:**

1. Resuming your loop road exploration, stop by more studios and galleries. The Cliff Dwellers Gallery, featuring work from over 60 local artists, is a must-see.

2. Visit the Alewine Leather studio to see the wonderful handcrafted leather goods they are famous for. Enjoy the fine craftsmanship and think about getting a special leather accessory or memento.

3. Discover the Smoky Mountain Cat House, a gallery featuring artwork and crafts inspired by cats. You can find a wide range of cat-themed items, from paintings to pottery, that are sure to please cat lovers.

4. As you travel the picturesque circular route, pause to observe the surrounding landscape. Enjoy the tranquil streams, lush forests, and stunning views of the Smoky Mountains in the area.

**Evening:**

1. If the Gatlinburg Arts and Crafts Community's annual Craftsmen's Fair is taking place while you're there, think about going. Live demonstrations, interactive workshops, and a wide variety of handcrafted goods are all available for purchase at this event, which is held at the Gatlinburg Convention Center.

2. At one of the Gatlinburg restaurants, indulge in a sumptuous meal to cap off your day excursion. Consider the inventiveness and brilliance you saw while investigating the arts and crafts loop.

3. If you have time, take a stroll along the Parkway in the heart of Gatlinburg and take in the town's vibrant ambiance, shops, and attractions.

# Chapter 11: Security And Safety

## 1. General Travel Tips:

There are several important factors for visitors to take into account when it comes to safety and security in Gatlinburg, a well-known tourist destination tucked away in the picturesque Smoky Mountains of Tennessee. It's critical to put your health first whether you're organizing a family vacation, a romantic retreat, or an exciting excursion. To assist you have a safe and secure trip to Gatlinburg, here are some general travel tips:

**1. Planning and research:**
Do an extensive study on the safety situation in Gatlinburg before your vacation, including any most recent updates or advisories. Learn the laws, traditions, and emergency contact information specific to the area. Consider the sights, events, and locations you want to visit when you plan your itinerary. Keep abreast of local weather forecasts as well as any potential natural disasters.

**2. Selection of Accommodations:**

Selecting reliable hotels, resorts, or vacation rentals with good reviews will help you have a successful trip. Places with good security features, such as well-lit parking lots, security cameras, and secure room access, should be given priority. Read up on safety features given by the property, such as in-room safes, and fire safety measures.

**3. Personal Belongings:**

Keep your personal belongings protected at all times. Invest in a solid travel lock or utilize the in-room safe to store valuable valuables such as passports, cash, and electronic gadgets when you're not using them. While exploring Gatlinburg, bring just essential belongings and avoid exhibiting expensive jewelry or big quantities of cash.

**4. Transportation:**

If you're traveling to Gatlinburg, ensure your vehicle is in good condition before going on your adventure. Familiarize yourself with the area traffic regulations, including speed limits and parking restrictions. When parking your vehicle, pick well-lit places or secure parking lots. If you want to take public transit or hire a taxi or ridesharing service, rely on licensed and trustworthy companies.

**5. Awareness of Surroundings:**
Maintain situational awareness throughout your time in Gatlinburg. Stay attentive and watchful of your surroundings, especially in crowded areas, tourist attractions, and public transportation hubs. Be aware of pickpockets and keep an eye on your stuff in busy places. Avoid giving sensitive personal information to strangers and be skeptical of unsolicited offers or pleas for assistance.

**6. Emergency Preparedness:**
Familiarize yourself with the nearest medical institutions, police stations, and fire stations in Gatlinburg. Keep emergency contact numbers ready on your phone and in a written format. Consider investing in travel insurance that covers medical emergencies, trip cancellations, and lost possessions. If you have any

specific medical conditions or allergies, carry the required medication and inform your travel companions.

**7. Outdoor Activities:**

Gatlinburg provides several outdoor activities like hiking, camping, and wildlife exploration. Before partaking in these activities, research and observe safety rules offered by the National Park Service and local authorities. Dress correctly for the weather, have extra water and snacks, and alert someone about your plans if heading into remote locations. Stay on defined pathways, avoid feeding wildlife, and be aware of potentially hazardous interactions, such as snakes or bears.

**8. Weather Considerations:**

Gatlinburg experiences diverse weather conditions throughout the year. Be prepared for rapid fluctuations in temperature, rain, or snowfall depending on the season. Monitor weather forecasts and advisories, especially if you plan to engage in outside activities. In case of severe weather warnings, follow local authorities' recommendations and take proper shelter.

**9. Health and Hygiene:**

Maintain proper hygiene standards during your visit to Gatlinburg. Wash your hands frequently, especially before eating, and carry hand sanitizer for instances when handwashing facilities are not readily available.

## 2. Security Precautions:

In addition to general travel advice, there are specific security precautions you may take to maximize your safety while visiting Gatlinburg. Here are some critical security measures to consider:

**1. Personal Safety:**

- Be cautious when walking alone, especially at night or in less-populated regions. Stick to well-lit and busy streets.

- Trust your instincts and avoid situations that feel unsafe or unpleasant.

- Stay in groups, if feasible, when exploring the town or participating in outdoor activities.

- Use approved walking roads and trails, and avoid straying into restricted or off-limits areas.

- Report any suspicious activities to the police or seek aid from local businesses or people if you feel intimidated or come across any questionable activity.

**2. Property Protection:**
- When departing, lock all of your accommodations' windows, doors, and balconies.

- Check someone out through the peephole or viewer before opening the door to them.

- Use the hotel's safe deposit boxes or keep your valuables locked up somewhere safe inside your lodging.

- Don't leave pricey stuff in your car while it's unattended. If necessary, lock them away, either in the trunk or elsewhere.

- If you're renting a vacation home, make sure the locks are safe and abide by any additional security instructions the owner or management may have given.

**3. Cybersecurity:**
- Only access personal or financial information online when using secure, password-protected Wi-Fi networks.

- Use caution while connecting to public Wi-Fi networks because hackers may be able to access them. Avoid using these networks to access or transact sensitive information.

- Always keep the most recent security software updated and password-protected on all of your electronic devices, including computers and cellphones.

- Avoid downloading files from dubious sources or clicking on questionable links.

- Be aware of your social media usage and refrain from posting about your absence from your lodging or particular vacation plans.

**4. Emergency Preparedness:**
- Learn the emergency evacuation protocols supplied by your lodging or local tourist information offices.

- Save emergency phone numbers in your phone's contacts and carry a physical copy of your important contacts' names and addresses.

- Be aware of any local weather warnings, safety alerts, or emergency alerts.

- Bring the essential medication and let your traveling partners know if you have any unique medical issues or allergies.

- In emergencies, such as those involving public safety or natural disasters, abide by local authority's orders.

**5. Public Events and Gatherings:**
- When you attend public gatherings, festivals, or events, pay attention to your surroundings and the dynamics of the crowd.

- Be on the lookout for any shady activity or unsecured baggage or shipments. Any worries should be reported right away to the police or the event security staff.

- Become familiar with the designated assembly areas and emergency exits in event locations.

Though Gatlinburg is generally a secure place to visit, it's still necessary to follow some security steps to guarantee a worry-free and pleasurable trip.

Made in the USA
Middletown, DE
11 July 2023

34869675R00126